Contents

The research on which this book is based was funded by an Adult Education Special Projects grant to Purdue University from the Indiana Department of Public Instruction.

Cover design by Boni Nash

Foreword

I n *Occupational Literacy Education,* Timothy Rush, Alden Moe, and Rebecca Storlie perform a needed service for educators everywhere. Most educators are aware that the workplace is changing and that service and technical professions are growing. Few educators are aware, in specific, of what this means for the adults and adolescents they teach. *Occupational Literacy Education* provides glimpses of the sorts of reading, writing, and oral language adults face during training and on the job for ten different occupations ranging from account clerk to auto mechanic to licensed practical nurse.

High school teachers and reading specialists may be surprised at the difficult and complex literacy tasks which will confront their noncollege-bound students. Students anxious to leave high school so they can escape reading and writing should be brought face to face with the reality of on-the-job and training reading materials gathered in *Occupational Literacy Education.* Reading specialists will want to share portions of the book with vocational education, science, mathematics, and business education teachers who can borrow ideas to improve the real world basic skills of their students.

Occupational Literacy Education also will be useful to adult educators. Teachers of adult basic education as well as teachers in job retraining programs will appreciate the book's concise synthesis of recent research on adult learning and on workplace literacy. The recommendations of applications oriented instructional methods presented in the fifth chapter are particularly useful. Many adult educators who prepare students to take high school equivalency examinations (GED) have complained about the dearth of job oriented literacy materials to help adults see the connection between their learning and a chance to get a good job and improve the quality of their lives. A mixture of GED materials and ideas from *Occupational Literacy Education* should provide a useful balance of learning experiences to keep adults motivated with practical reading tasks while they are also preparing for the less immediate academic reading tasks on the GED examination.

I have shared portions of this text with a number of experienced teachers. For many, the last direct experience with nonteaching work was a summer job held years ago during college days. Most are startled by the wide gap between their own memories of simple job literacy tasks of a decade or more ago and the complexities of the ten occupations studied by Rush and his colleagues. This startling glimpse of current workplace reality may, in the final analysis, be the most valuable contribution of *Occupational Literacy Education*.

Larry Mikulecky
Indiana University
Bloomington, Indiana

Preface

T his book has been prepared for a varied audience of educators. Our primary goal, however, has been to provide adult and occupational educators with basic information for developing literacy and related occupational competencies. Chapters 1 through 4 present foundational knowledge as a basis for instruction.

We believe that teachers at every level of the educational process should recognize the value of applying literacy and literacy related competencies in work related contexts. Recommendations of applications oriented instructional methods are made in Chapter 5.

The vocabulary of work, with its combination of purely technical and multiple meaning words, should provide a basis for instruction in reading and basic occupational knowledge. Chapter 6 is devoted to methods of vocabulary development and lists of high frequency and technical words are presented in the Appendices.

Finally, we are grateful to our students, colleagues, and reviewers who have questioned our ideas and critiqued our work. Since this project began with all three authors working together in Indiana, and has been completed with the authors working in Wyoming, Louisiana, and Minnesota, respectively, it is difficult to recognize all who have helped. Nevertheless, we express thanks to the many individuals who contributed.

RTR
AJM
RLS

1

Introduction to *Occupational Literacy Education*

P reparing people for success in occupational roles is a complex and difficult process. Functional competencies must be developed in critical areas ranging from affective characteristics, manual arts, and technical knowledge to mathematics, written language, and oral language. This book focuses on the development of written and oral language competencies required in occupational and training settings. Occupational literacy and the literacy competencies necessary for success in work and training environments are described. Building on the summary of human cognition, we offer instructional recommendations for developing occupational literacy and related competencies. The last chapter is devoted to methods of vocabulary development, and may be used in conjunction with the technical vocabularies listed in the Appendices.

The ability to competently read required, work related materials is defined here as *occupational literacy*. This definition, based on a concept of functional literacy (Kirsch & Guthrie, 1977-1978), is limited to competence with printed materials of all sorts. By definition, functional literacy varies according to individual demands of divergent roles, settings, and materials. Occupational literacy competencies comprise a subset of functional literacy. Required competencies vary from occupation to occupation and from job to job within occupations.

Occupational literacy development is an important aspect of prevocational, vocational, and on-the-job education. Occupational literacy related linguistic competencies — writing and oral language — also require instructional attention.

1

Literacy and Work

Until recently, little research has been done on the subject of work related literacy. The lack of information about the literacy requirements of specific occupations has been cited (Kirsch & Guthrie, 1977-1978; Sticht, 1980) as a serious obstruction to the development of effective occupational and literacy training programs. In their review of literacy programs in industrial, military, and penal settings, Ryan and Furlong (1975) noted only scattered reports related to the literacy requirements of industrial occupations. Systematic analysis of the literacy requirements of jobs, though relatively easy to conduct, has received little attention from researchers. Ryan and Furlong argued that, although many programs intended to improve adult literacy have been motivated by economic interests, the lack of research on occupational literacy makes it impossible to know if literacy training has any effect on successful employment.

Research on occupational literacy, sponsored largely by the United States Armed Forces, has provided insight about the extent to which reading is used in work and training settings and the nature of reading tasks in those settings. Sticht (1975) reported that incumbents in military jobs are consistently confronted with reading tasks which average two hours per work day. In the same report, Sticht noted that the difficulty of required reading materials often exceeded the measured reading abilities of successful workers. Kern (1970) observed results similar to those noted by Sticht. Disparities between reading requirements and reading abilities resulted in the disuse of technical manuals by military technicians.

In an examination of reading in the Navy, Sticht et al. (1977a) distinguished between two dominant uses of reading in occupational settings; *reading-to-do* tasks differ from *reading-to-learn* tasks in that the former are used to accomplish work while the latter involve retention of information for later use. According to this research, 75 percent of the reading tasks done by military personnel involve reading-to-do. In these tasks, written and graphic information is referred to and used, but is not learned. Sticht also noted that 1) materials encountered in reading-to-do are rarely unfamiliar to the worker; 2) such materials are commonly reread on a daily basis; and 3) the permanence of printed materials enables them to serve as a kind of external memory for workers.

A second study by Sticht et al. (1977b) analyzed reading-to-do tasks required of Navy personnel in ten occupations and training programs. The authors reported that fact finding and following directions are the most frequent reading-to-do tasks. Job related reading typically involves finding facts or following directions presented in combined graphic and text formats. Workers and instructors used fact finding skills twice as often as they used skills in following directions; students used following directions skills twice as much as fact finding skills.

Literacy research on civilian occupations is less plentiful than research involving military occupations. Recent studies, however, indicate that the requirements of civilian occupations are similar to those of military occupations. Diehl and Mikulecky (1980) reported that, for a broad cross section of occupations, daily reading is almost universally required.

The amount of time spent on daily occupational reading in civilian contexts is substantial. In describing the reading habits of adults, Sharon (1973-1974) reported a median of 61 minutes spent on work related reading tasks. Mikulecky, Shanklin, and Caverly (1979) reported a mean of 73 minutes per day of work related reading. Diehl (1980) observed a mean work related reading time of 113 minutes per day. Diehl's figure is similar to the two hours per day reported by Sticht (1975) for military occupations.

Sticht et al. (1977a) and Diehl and Mikulecky (1980) called attention to important differences between the reading materials and processes observed in occupational settings compared to materials and processes observed in school settings. Reading-to-do tasks occur in about the same proportion in civilian occupational reading as in military contexts; reading-to-learn predominates in civilian occupational training settings.

In suggesting reasons why civilian and military workers can cope with reading demands which exceed their abilities, Diehl (1980) and Diehl and Mikulecky note the highly repetitive nature of on-the-job reading tasks and the influence of worker interest, motivation, experience, and specialized knowledge. They emphasize that workers can use extralinguistic cues (equipment and tools) to aid understanding. Diehl, however, observed that it may be inappropriate to view on-the-job reading materials as indicators of literacy demands, suggesting that such materials reflect only "opportunities" to use reading as a tool for increasing job efficiency and success. In most cases, workers have recourse to other sources (supervisors and co-workers, for instance) of necessary information.

Writing and Other Competencies

Diehl (1980) reported that in 64.7 percent of occupational writing examined, the task involved completing simple forms or preparing brief memoranda. Writing tasks were repeated frequently enough for workers to master the most complex forms. Memoranda were simple, concise, and relatively easy to write. Diehl suggested that further research may show that writing competencies required for successful job performance are simple, and unrelated to the writing tasks observed in schools.

The nature of listening competencies required at work has received little attention from researchers. Sticht (1975), however, described studies which show that military personnel learn equally well through listening or reading and noted that it is possible for such personnel to learn from tape recordings played at accelerated rates.

A general sense of the importance of listening skills in occupational settings can be inferred from studies of adults in general. Rankin's study (1926) indicated that 70 percent of daily adult activities involve oral communication and 45 percent of communication involves listening. The amount of oral communication time typical of occupations varies considerably, but it seems likely that about 50 percent of such time requires listening.

It might also be inferred that the nature of reading and listening tasks in on-the-job and school settings is similar. Possible parallels between occupational listening and reading competencies, however, require examination through research.

Summary

Research dealing with the literacy competencies of occupations and training programs indicates that:

- reading tasks are part of virtually all occupations studied;
- workers perform reading tasks for major portions of the work day;
- reading materials and processes observed in work settings are distinctly different from those found in school settings; and
- occupational materials are successfully read by workers who seem to lack the necessary reading abilities.

Little is known about competencies related to occupational literacy. While writing tasks seem to be brief and highly repetitive in nature, occupational uses of oral language remain largely unexamined.

References

Diehl, W.A. *Functional literacy as a variable construct: An examination of attitudes, behaviors, and strategies related to occupational literacy.* Doctoral dissertation, Indiana University, 1980.

Diehl, W.A., and Mikulecky, L. The nature of reading at work. *Journal of Reading,* 1980, *24,* 221-227.

Kern, R.P. *Readability, reading ability, and readership.* Alexandria, VA: Human Resources Research Organization, 1970.

Kirsch, I., and Guthrie, J.T. The concept and measurement of functional literacy. *Reading Research Quarterly,* 1977-1978, *13,* 485-507.

Mikulecky, L.J., Shanklin, N.L., and Caverly, D.C. *Adult reading habits, attitudes, and motivations: A cross sectional study.* Monograph in Language and Reading Series, No. 2. Bloomington, IN: School of Education, Indiana University, 1979.

Rankin, P. *The measurement of the ability to understand spoken language.* Doctoral dissertation, University of Michigan, 1926.

Ryan, T.A., and Furlong, W. Literacy programs in industry, the armed forces, and penal institutions. In J.B. Carroll and J.S. Chall (Eds.), *Toward a literate society.* New York: McGraw-Hill, 1975.

Sharon, A. What do adults read? *Reading Research Quarterly,* 1973-1974, *9,* 148-169.

Sticht, T.G. *Reading for working: A functional literacy anthology.* Alexandria, VA: Human Resources Research Organization, 1975.

Sticht, T.G. Minimum competency in functional literacy for work. In R.M. Jaeger and C.K. Tittle (Eds.), *Minimum competency achievement testing.* Berkeley, CA: McCutchan, 1980.

Sticht, T.G., Fox, L., Hauke, R., and Zaph, D. *The role of reading in the navy* NPRDC TR *77-77.* San Diego, CA: Navy Personnel Research and Development Center, 1977a.

Sticht, T.G., Fox, L., Hauke, R., and Zaph, D. *Integrated job skills and reading skills training program.* San Diego, CA: Navy Personnel Research Development Center, 1977b.

2

Studies of Occupational Literacy Requirements

The studies which form the basis of this book were conducted in response to a need expressed by employment and guidance counselors, adult educators, and students in adult basic education, for information about the literacy demands of specific occupations. The occupations studied are frequently chosen as career goals by adult basic education students. Officials of educational and social service agencies confirmed the need to examine the following ten occupations:

Account Clerk	Industrial Maintenance
Auto Mechanic	Mechanic
Draftsman	Licensed Practical Nurse
Electrician	Machine Tool Operator
Heating/Air Conditioning	Secretary
Mechanic	Welder

Goals

While the work of researchers such as those cited previously has contributed to important knowledge about the nature of occupational reading requirements and abilities, much indepth study of reading and other linguistic requirements of work remains to be done. Knowledge of such factors, their interrelatedness, and their effects on job performance are essential to those concerned with prevocational, vocational, and on-the-job training.

The goals of the studies discussed here were to 1) identify the reading, writing, listening, and speaking competencies required in ten skilled and semiskilled occupations; 2) compare those requirements with those in corresponding vocational training programs; and 3) evaluate the relative importance of the identified competencies to successful job performance.

Definitions and Assumptions

Occupational literacy, like functional literacy, can be a confusing concept. Functional literacy, for example, has been defined to include speaking, listening, writing, and computational competencies. Job success depends on many levels of competence. In occupational settings, job knowledge, experience, dependability, motivation, cooperativeness, and perseverance are important cognitive and affective qualities. Though not directly involved with literacy, competence with language and numerical processes is often necessary for successful job performance.

As mentioned earlier, the definition of occupational literacy used in these studies—functional competence in reading job related materials—was derived from Kirsch and Guthrie (1977-1978) who proposed that functional literacy be defined according to the demands of specific situations in terms of competency in reading alone. In their view, listening, speaking, writing, and computation involve functional cognitive competence. In these studies, listening, speaking, and writing were defined as literacy related competencies.

The following assumptions prompted and guided the investigations.

1. Reading, writing, listening, and speaking competencies are essential to worker success in the occupations examined.
2. Job supervisors view occupational literacy and related competencies as essential to successful worker performance.
3. Successful workers view occupational literacy and related competencies as essential to successful job performance.
4. Higher levels of literacy and literacy related competencies are required for success in occupational training programs than are necessary for success on the job.
5. The literacy and literacy related competencies required for success on the job and in vocational training programs are attainable by adults whose levels of literacy place them in adult basic education programs.

Population

The population in each study represented two groups, workers at job sites and students in training program courses. For each of the ten occupational categories, three job sites and three courses from a related training program curriculum were studied.

The thirty job sites studied were selected at random from an exhaustive list of employees representing a broad spectrum of business and industry in the greater Lafayette, Indiana (population approximately 115,000), area. At each job site, one worker and an immediate supervisor were involved. Workers were selected from pools of employees who had spent a minimum of six months on the job and who were judged by their employers to be functioning successfully in their work roles.

For each occupational category, three courses from a corresponding postsecondary vocational training program were studied. For the categories of electrician and heating/air conditioning mechanic, one course from an appropriate trade union apprenticeship program was studied. Each occupational category was involved with three courses from the curriculum of a state supported, postsecondary occupational training program. A total of twenty-five different courses were studied because the curricula of several of the occupational training programs had common course requirements.

Data Collection

Methods of data collection were similar in both job site and occupational training settings. Two thousand word samples of required reading materials were obtained from job site and occupational training program courses, including samples of textbooks, technical manuals, handbooks, instructional manuals for the installation and repair of equipment, memoranda and checklists written in informal and nonstandard English, and diagrams accompanied by clarifying words and phrases. When possible, passages were selected from materials according to the guidelines of the Dale-Chall (Dale & Chall, 1948) readability formula and the Fry Readability Graph (Fry, 1977). When samples were too brief for such guidelines to apply, entire samples were transcribed and analyzed. Some of the samples, such as memoranda and diagrams, were inappropriate for valid evaluation with the readability formulas used; such samples were, however, included as part of the corpus of language used to establish occupational vocabulary lists which appear in the appendices of this book.

Oral language requirements of the occupations studied were obtained by tape recording the oral language of workers or instructors and their coworkers or students during a typical one hour period of a workday. Oral language samples from training programs included both classroom and laboratory settings. Language recorded in this way was subsequently transcribed and keypunched for computer analysis.

Writing samples produced by workers and students in conjunction with their work and training activities were collected at each site.

Data Analysis Procedures

To determine the readability of required reading materials from the job and occupational training program sites, two well-known instruments were used. The Dale-Chall formula and the Fry Readability Graph were programed in the FORTRAN language compatible with the Purdue University CDC 6600 mainframe computer. Each sample of required reading material was analyzed with both readability instruments. The readability results for each of the materials were then used to establish a readability range for work and training materials for each occupation.

Reading materials were examined with respect to the way in which they were used on site. Sticht's distinction (1975) between purposes for reading guided this aspect of the studies. The degree to which reading was used to accomplish work or to learn information was evaluated. Reading-to-do as opposed to reading-to-learn distinctions were made for required reading at each job and training program site. All required reading materials from job and training program sites were rated according to the level of formality of usage in which they were written.

Tape recordings of oral language produced on the job were transcribed and visually analyzed to establish the general level of English usage (Pooley, 1974).

Writing samples collected at each of the sites were evaluated for level of usage; legibility; and special characteristics such as inclusion of diagrams, sketches, and other aids to reader comprehension. Written and oral language samples were then combined. Computer programs were used to prepare technical vocabulary lists for each occupation as well as lists of the highest frequency words for each occupation and for the entire language sample.

Results of the studies are discussed in the following chapter.

References

Dale, E., and Chall, J. A formula for predicting readability. *Educational Research Bulletin,* 1948, *27,* 37-54.

Fry, E. Fry's readability graph: Clarifications, validity, and extension to level 17. *Journal of Reading,* 1977, *21,* 242-252.

Kirsch, I., and Guthrie, J. The concept and measurement of functional literacy. *Reading Research Quarterly,* 1977-1978, *13,* 485-507.

Pooley, R. *The teaching of English usage.* Urbana, IL: National Council of Teachers of English, 1974.

Sticht, T. Reading for working: A functional literacy anthology. Alexandria, VA: Human Resources Research Organization, 1975.

3
Literacy Competencies in Ten Occupations

T his chapter presents and discusses the findings of studies of the reading, writing, and oral language requirements of the ten occupations and related training programs described in Chapter 2. The studies focused on the importance of reading to job performance, the amount of time spent reading, and how reading was used on the job. Reading and literacy related competencies necessary to successful job performance were examined through analysis of sample reading materials, handwritten communications, and tape recordings.

Data on competences required for success in occupational training programs were obtained through observations and from samples of reading, writing, and oral language from the curriculum of relevant vocational college programs.

On the Job

Literacy Requirements

Work related reading was performed daily by each of the workers involved in the studies. Consistent with the findings of Diehl (1980), Table 1 shows that reading was universally required of those studied, though there were variations in time spent reading and the nature of the reading task.

Table 1

SUMMARY OF ON-THE-JOB READING

Occupation	Average Daily Reading Time (minutes)	Type Material	Readability Score	Use	Frequency	Prose Style
Account Clerk	120	Correspondence, ledgers, lists, tables	Grade 13 to College Grad	To do	Daily	Informal, formal
Auto Mechanic	60	Technical references, memos, work orders	Grade 10 to College Grad	To learn, to do	Daily	Informal, formal
Draftsman	45	Technical references, blueprints, code books, reference books, memos	Grade 10 to College Grad	To do	Daily	Informal, formal
Electrician	120	Technical references, blueprints, schematics	College Graduate	To do	Daily	Informal, formal, technical
Heating/Air Conditioning Mechanic	45	Manuals, blueprints, memos	Grade 10 to College Grade	To learn, to do	Daily	Informal, formal

Industrial Maintenance Mechanic	42	Service manuals, handbooks, operating manuals, memos, workorders	Grade 10 to College Grad	To learn, to do	Daily	Informal, technical
Licensed Practical Nurse	78	Charts, tables, card files, handbooks, reference books	Grade 10 to College Junior	To learn, to do	Daily, weekly	Informal, formal
Machine Tool Operator	36	Manuals, handbooks, checklists, memos	Grade 9 to College Grad	To do	Daily	Informal, technical
Secretary	168	Reference books, tables, lists, letters, handbooks, memos	Grade 16 to College Grad	To do	Daily	Informal, formal
Welder	24	Blueprints, tables, memos	N/A	To do	Daily	Informal

Workers reported that they sometimes reread the same material several times per workday, and that such repetition was necessary. Repeated reading was recognized as a means of avoiding costly memory related errors. Workers' statements reflected the consistent view that careful readings of checklists, instructions, and directions were necessary to job success and security. For example, when asked if careless reading of on-the-job materials could affect work, a draftsman replied, "Definitely! The entire reliability of our finished product may rely on proper sizes and testing requirements derived from [reading] the [building] code."

The average time spent reading work related materials during the workday was 66 minutes, with a range of 24 minutes to 4 hours per day. This average reading time is similar to the 61 minutes reported by Sharon (1973). Studies by Diehl (1980) and Sticht (1975) found that workers engaged in work related reading for approximately 2 hours per day.

The difference between the findings of Diehl and Sticht compared to those of Sharon and the studies discussed here may be due to the use of differing definitions of reading. Lacking a comprehensive definition of reading, workers and supervisors probably did not include time spent reading information in formats other than printed discourse; the use of labels, tables, charts, figures, blueprints, schematics and checklists, may not have been considered aspects of reading. In fact, all of these studies may underestimate the actual amount of reading done by workers. Recent research by Mikulecky (1982) indicates that workers themselves underestimated by an average of 45 percent the amount of time they spent reading.

Reading-to-do work was the predominant use of reading in all occupations. Only licensed practical nurses and industrial maintenance mechanics reported reading on the job in order to learn information. Nevertheless, in these, as in the other occupations, reading-to-do was the dominant use of reading. Similar findings were obtained by Diehl (1980) and Sticht (1975) who, respectively, reported that reading-to-do constituted 66 percent and 75 percent of on-the-job reading.

Reading materials encountered by workers participating in the studies discussed here were varied in length, type, level of usage, and format. Table 1 reflects this diversity. Materials included single page memoranda, forms, procedural checklists, and lengthy handbooks. Memoranda and forms often employed informal, truncated usage. Example 1 presents samples from the account clerk and machine tool operator occupations which are typical of materials found in all occupations studied.

Example 1. Informal styles of reading materials: Account clerk and machine tool operator.

Account Clerk

1. Check paid invoice file.
2. Check completed purchase order.
3. Go back to original receiving order.
4. Check current invoice file.

Machine Tool Operator

1. Clean shavings from table.
2. Release locating pilots and clamp.
3. Remove pieces and lay them aside.
4. Position clamp bar, align stops, partly secure clamps.

The level of longer documents was generally formal, highly technical, and complex. Workers frequently were required to read texts such as those shown in Example 2.

Example 2. Technical styles of reading materials: Heating/air conditioning and nursing.

Heating/Air Conditioning

Room thermostats and remote bulb insertion and immersion thermostats shall be two pipe, of the proportional relay type, except where two positioned action is necessary, and the temperature settings and reset ranges shall be adjustable to best meet the actual operation conditions.

Nursing

Attached to the trachea, this gland is located beneath the larynx and above the sternum. It is U-shaped (two lobes connected by an isthmus) and secretes a hormone called *thyroxine*.

Rating of the English used in materials read by workers on the job was done using Pooley's varieties (1974) of English usage. For all occupations, except welder, the range of usage varied from nonstandard, informal, and ungrammatical through formal and highly technical.

The format of on-the-job reading materials, whether informal or formal and technical in style, usually involved graphic presentation of information. Tables, charts, graphs and figures appeared both in conjunction with and apart from written text. Workers were required to find and interpret such combinations of text and graphic information to perform daily routines. Skill in reading graphic information in formats such as those shown in Examples 3 and 4 is an important occupational literacy competency.

Example 3. Text and graphic format.

Textual Format

Inspection Openings
  All pressure vessels for use with compressed air, except as permitted otherwise in this paragraph, and those subjected to internal corrosion, or having parts subject to erosion or mechanical abrasion (see UG-25) shall be provided with a suitable manhole, handhole, or other inspection opening for examination and cleaning. (Pressure Vessel Codebook, p. 42)

Tabled Information

	Type 1	Type II			Type III		Type IV	Type V	
	Noncombustible				Combustible				
Building Element	Fire Resistive	Fire Resistive	1 Hr.	N	1 Hr.	N	M.T.	1 Hr.	N
Exterior Bearing Walls	4 Sec. 1803 (a)	4 1903 (a)	1	N	4 2103 (a)	4 2103 (a)	4 2103 (a)	1	N
Interior Bearing Walls	3	2	1	N	1	N	1	1	N
Exterior Nonbearing Walls	4 Sec. 1803 (a)	4 1903 (a)	1	N	4 2103 (a)	4 2103 (a)	4 2103 (a)	1	N

(Uniform Building Code)

Graphic formats involving illustrations were found in each occupation. Example 4 shows a typical illustration.

Technical vocabulary presented special demands to workers in each occupation. Necessary words were sometimes purely technical, having single occupation specific meanings. More often workers had to recognize the occupational meanings of everyday words with multiple meanings.

Example 4. Typical illustration.

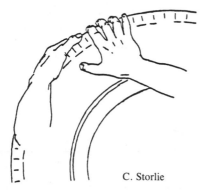

Wheel bearing adjustment can be checked by a push-pull procedure. Place one hand at ten o'clock on the outboard side of the tire. Place the other hand on the inside. Push and pull. Note any play. Adjust as necessary.

C. Storlie

Placement of Hands in Checking Wheel Bearing Play

Literacy Related Requirements

Samples of written language from the studies revealed that only rudimentary skills were required. When Pooley's criteria (1974) for levels of English usage were applied to the writing produced at job sites, distinctions between printed and handwritten prose were clearly evident. Whereas the level of printed reading materials was usually formal and highly technical, handwritten materials were informally written and could sometimes be classified as nonstandard English. The secretarial occupation stood alone in requiring a formal level of writing.

Clarity was the chief requirement of on-the-job writing. Typical handwritten communications were done in concise, ungrammatical, nonstandard English containing only essential information. Messages and memoranda omitted articles (a, an, the) and resembled the style of English found in telegrams. Example 5 shows typical written communications from occupational settings.

Example 5. On-the-job writing.
Nature of Trouble: Two lights out.
Action Taken:
1. Replaced tube in one light fixture.
2. Replaced ballast in light fixture.
   Light operating now, but still needs new ceramic end connection.

Diversity of legibility in handwriting was tolerated as long as it did not detract from communication of important information. In most occupations, workers produced scripts which would probably be considered marginal by elementary and secondary school standards. Higher standards of legibility were expected in the drafting and secretarial occupations in which quality of handwriting represented the employer to outsiders.

Oral Language

Oral language use on the job involved the production and interpretation of clear but informally constructed English utterances. Much language encountered was social and not directly related to work. When talk was work related, it focused on specific tasks, tools, and equipment.

Speakers often worked at being understood—repeating, rewording, referring to similar tasks, and demonstrating as necessary. Listeners questioned, restated instructions, and acted out tasks to make sure they understood what they had heard. Then they acted on the information and instructions they had heard. Example 6 presents typical work related conversation.

Example 6. Work related oral language.

Account Clerk

"I think the credit is more than the debit. We would end up not writing a check, because we would get a debit from them for thirty-three eighty-four for two of these. We paid them because they gave us past due notices on them and Jones-Perkins finally put them through."

Secretary

"Yes, may I talk to Mr. Jones, please? I'm calling in reference to your telephone etiquette seminar. We don't have enough people to hold the class, so we're going to have to cancel."

Except in the secretarial jobs, in which formal usage was frequently employed, an informal level of usage typified on-the-job oral language. Clarity of communication was clearly more important than what might be termed "good grammar."

The Training Programs

Literacy Requirements

Reading was a daily requirement of students in all training program courses associated with the ten occupations. As in the research reported by Sticht (1975) and Mikulecky (1982), reading was required in both training and work settings, but the nature of reading differed in these settings.

In contrast to the job sites where reading-to-do prevailed, reading-to-learn was dominant in the training programs. In reading-to-do, short term memory serves to temporarily store the information for immediate use. In reading-to-learn, short term memory functions to organize information for storage in long term memory.

Compared to workers, students spent much more time per day reading. During the school day and after hours, students read in classroom and laboratory situations, as well as during periods of independent study. Student reading, as estimated by instructors, ranged from forty-two minutes to six hours per day. Table 2 shows the estimated reading load for training programs corresponding to each occupation studied. The actual reading time for individual students was probably greater than the estimates shown. The table shows ranges based on estimates from three courses; most students were enrolled in more than three courses.

Reading in the training programs required extensive use of expository and descriptive prose. Textbooks, reference books, and sets of complex instructions were part of the daily required reading. In most required reading, students carefully studied and learned the information presented in text, graphic, and text/graphic formats similar to those found at the job sites.

Book length materials were used by students in classroom, laboratory, and independent study. Shorter materials in the form of quizzes, instruction sets, and chalkboard notes written by instructors were frequently encountered in the school settings. These materials, too, presented information in combinations of text and graphic formats.

The usage observed in the required reading materials was varied. As with materials from the job sites, styles ranged from informal and ungrammatical to formal, highly technical prose. Example 7 shows instances of informal and technical usage.

Table 2

SUMMARY OF TRAINING PROGRAM READING

Occupation	Average Daily Reading Time (minutes)	Type Material	Readability Score	Use	Frequency	Prose Style
Account Clerk	187	Textbooks, references, ledgers, chalkboard notes	Grade 11 to College Grad	To learn, to do	Daily	Informal, formal, technical
Auto Mechanic	108	Textbooks, references, figures, tables, chalkboard notes	Grade 9 to College Grad	To learn, to do	Daily	Informal, formal, technical
Draftsman	174	Textbooks, references, blueprints, figures, tables	Grade 9 to College Grad	To learn, to do	Daily	Informal, formal, technical
Electrician	280	Textbooks, references, figures, tables, chalkboard notes	Grade 10 to College Grad	To learn, to do	Daily	Informal, formal, technical
Heating/Air Conditioning Mechanic	120	Textbooks, references, figures, tables, blueprints	Grade 11 to College Grad	To learn, to do	Daily	Informal, formal, technical

Occupational Literacy Education

Industrial Maintenance Mechanic	300	Textbooks, references, figures, tables, blueprints	Grade 10 to College Grad	To learn, to do	Daily	Informal, formal, technical
Licensed Practical Nurse	360	Textbooks, references, figures, tables, charts, procedures	Grade 12 to College Grad	To learn, to do	Daily	Informal, formal, technical
Machine Tool Operator	60	Textbooks, references, figures, tables, blueprints	Grade 9 to College Grad	To learn, to do	Daily	Informal, formal, technical
Secretary	280	Textbooks, references, figures, tables	Grade 10 to College Grad	To learn, to do	Daily	Informal, formal, technical
Welder	187	Textbooks, references, blueprints, figures, tables	Grade 8 to College Grad	To learn, to do	Daily	Informal, formal, technical

Example 7. Informal and technical usage.

Informal

Instructor (referring to a chalkboard diagram)

"Let's go back to those...to what's happening inside that stator winding. We've got a rotor with magnetic poles rotating. Right? Okay, what happens when all of a sudden we've got no magnetic load? Here we were inducing some current and now we don't have anything to induce against...."

Technical

Specifications

Work required for installation of electrical rough-in in precast concrete slabs.
1. In general, the electrical contractor shall
   * Provide all layout of holes through the precast concrete slabs to the general contractor for approval by the precaster.
   * Core drill through the voids in the precast slabs for installation of conduits and boxes.
   * Conceal all conduits for lighting, outlets, etc., in the fill above the precast concrete slabs.

In each of the training programs, a specialized vocabulary was present. Words which made up these technical vocabularies took two forms. True technical words, peculiar to each occupation, formed one class of technical vocabulary; the second component involved everyday words with special occupational meanings. Mastery of both types of technical vocabulary was essential to student success.

Writing

In occupational training, writing took the form of note taking and writing examinations and assignments. In all cases, accuracy of information was more important than standard English usage. Instructional emphasis on grammatical correctness was present in the secretarial courses, but was not apparent in other courses. There was similarity between training program and on-the-job requirements in this regard; only when poor writing interfered with clear communication was it considered a problem. Example 8 shows samples of written language produced by training program students.

Example 8. Typical student writing.

Examination Questions

Automotive Mechanic

Question: One cause of failure of an engine to start is?
Response: Wet distributor.

Welder

Question: What is the function of a regulator?
Response: Controls gas flow.

Handwriting produced by students, like that produced by workers, was often marginally legible. As with grammar and usage, poor handwriting was accepted unless it caused communication problems.

Oral Language

Oral language in training program classrooms and laboratories was less social than was the case at the job sites. Instructor-to-student and student-to-student interaction during formal meetings was consistently subject oriented.

The level of oral language usage during instruction was typically informal. Instructors did not read from prepared notes during lectures; their language was repetitive and often conversational as they presented and demonstrated concepts and methods.

Student talk during instructional sessions was normally restricted to brief questions and responses to questions. When directed toward peers, student talk was informal, but predominantly task oriented. Like those of their instructors, student utterances were informal and sometimes nonstandard. Example 9 shows excerpts of classroom and laboratory talk.

Example 9. Classroom oral language.
Heating/Air Conditioning Mechanic

Instructor: Does anybody need help getting started? Do you want to go through the problem where you find static?
Student: I have a question. Can you run your bathroom — our small bathroom — and the utility together?
Instructor: No. The proper way to do that is to put the utility room separate from the kitchen.

Electrician

Instructor: A thousand? Okay, a mill is going back to being one hundredth of a cent. It's going back to like property tax. Like one tenth of a cent, there are one hundred cents in a dollar. So, one tenth of one hundredth is what a thousand mills to a dollar is. It goes back to a tax rate.

Note taking was an important adjunct to listening in all training programs. Students regularly took notes during instructional sessions, those notes were similar to other forms of occupational writing produced by students and workers – informal and marginally legible.

Occupational Literacy and Readability Estimates

Readability refers to ease of understanding or comprehension of written text. Readability formulas have been developed to gauge the appropriateness of written materials for intended audiences. Popular formulas address two text based factors – sentence complexity and vocabulary diversity – in predicting readability. The Dale-Chall Formula (1948) and Fry Readability Graph (1977) were used to assess the difficulty of required reading material in these studies.

The scores of these formula methods require careful interpretation because text understandability or comprehensibility can be influenced by nontext factors such as reader interest and motivation, familiarity with text, task repetition, and the availability of information from graphics and other sources. Nontext factors may reduce the effective difficulty of any given text. The moderating effects of these factors are probably reflected in studies such as one by Sacher and Duffy (1978), who found that workers were capable of using information obtained from materials two grade levels above the measured reading abilities of the workers.

It seems likely that the scores of the Dale-Chall formula and the Fry Graph overestimate the reading skill levels necessary for successful performance by workers and students. It is not that these instruments were in error; they are widely used and accepted tools. However, they are among the popular readability formulas which rely solely on easily quantifiable aspects of printed materials. In occupational reading, whether on the job or during training, nontext factors enable workers and students to understand material which would be incomprehensible to persons who are disinterested, unmotivated, or unfamiliar with the subject matter and nontext sources of information.

While teachers can have confidence in readability formulas as predictors of general levels of text comprehensibility, the limitations of formulas must be borne in mind. Many factors which contribute to the comprehension of written text are not assessed by formulas and some of these factors can be addressed instructionally. Methods of developing occupational reading skills during preoccupational and occupational training are described in Chapter 5.

Summary

Literacy and literacy related competencies were required in each of the workplace and training program settings examined in studies of ten occupations. Reading, writing, and oral language were used to meet work and training requirements by all workers and students who participated.

Work related reading involved slightly more than an hour a day on the job and more than twice that time in the training program. Reading materials were written in several varieties, ranging from informal to formal, technical styles. Important information was presented in text, graphic, and combinations of text/graphic formats. Readability formulas indicated high levels of text difficulty.

The difficulty of reading requirements was moderated by the nature of reading in occupational settings. On the job, reading involved repetitive use of the same materials from day to day. Once mastered, apparently difficult reading materials seemed inconsequential. Training program reading involved vocabulary, concepts, and information formats which were introduced and mediated through the instructional process. Like workers, students probably faced less severe reading demands than formula scores suggest.

Literacy related competencies—writing and oral language communication—required only rudimentary skills. Written communications, on the job and in the training programs, typically employed nonstandard or informal usage. Marginally legible handwriting was accepted in most work and training settings. Nonstandard usage and marginal handwriting were accepted unless they interfered with clear communication.

In oral language, clarity of expression, not standard English usage, was the criterion for competence. Speakers and listeners needed to be concerned about understanding, not usage.

The reading demands of the occupations examined were probably overestimated. The methods used to assess readability did not account for worker/student familiarity with the vocabulary and concepts found in required reading materials. The repetitive nature of on-the-job reading was not considered during the assessment of readability.

References

Dale, E., and Chall, J. A formula for predicting readability. *Educational Research Bulletin*, 1948, *27*, 37-54.

Diehl, W. *Functional literacy as a variable construct: An examination of attitudes, behaviors, and strategies related to occupational literacy.* Doctoral dissertation, Indiana University, 1980.

Diehl, W., and Mikulecky, L. The nature of reading at work. *Journal of Reading*, 1980, *24*, 221-227.

Fry, E.P. Fry's readability graph: Clarifications, validity, and extension to level 17. *Journal of Reading*, 1977, *21*, 242-252.

Kirsch, I., and Guthrie, J. The concept and measurement of functional literacy. *Reading Research Quarterly*, 1977-1978, *13*, 485-507.

Mikulecky, L. Job literacy: The relationship between school preparation and workplace actuality. *Reading Research Quarterly*, 1982, *17*, 400-419.

Moe, A.J., Rush, R.T., and Storlie, R.L. *The literacy requirements of an account clerk on the job and in a vocational training program.* 1980. (CS 005 248)

Moe, A.J., Rush, R.T., and Storlie, R.L. *The literacy requirements of an automotive mechanic on the job and in a vocational training program.* 1980. (CS 005 251)

Moe, A.J., Rush, R.T., and Storlie, R.L. *The literacy requirements of a draftsman on the job and in a vocational training program.* 1980. (CS 005 250)

Moe, A.J., Rush, R.T., and Storlie, R.L. *The literacy requirements of an electrician on the job and in a vocational training program.* 1980 (CS 005 252)

Moe, A.J., Rush, R.T., and Storlie, R.L. *The literacy requirements of a heating and air conditioning mechanic on the job and in a vocational training program.* 1980. (ED 179 918)

Moe, A.J., Rush, R.T., and Storlie, R.L. *The literacy requirements of an industrial maintenance mechanic on the job and in a vocational training program.* 1980. (CS 005 254)

Moe, A.J., Rush, R.T., and Storlie, R.L. *The literacy requirements of a licensed practical nurse on the job and in a vocational training program.* 1979. (ED 179 917)

Moe, A.J., Rush, R.T., and Storlie, R.L. *The literacy requirements of a machine tool operator on the job and in a vocational training program.* 1980. (CS 005 247)

Moe, A.J., Rush, R.T., and Storlie, R.L. *The literacy requirements of a secretary on the job and in a vocational training program.* 1980. (cs 005 249)

Moe, A.J., Rush, R.T., and Storlie, R.L. *The literacy requirements of a welder on the job and in a vocational training program.* 1980. (cs 005 253)

Pooley, R. *The teaching of English usage.* Urbana, IL: National Council of Teachers of English, 1974.

Sacher, J., and Duffy, T. *Reading skill and military effectiveness.* Paper presented at the meeting of the American Educational Research Association, Toronto, 1978. (ED 151 745)

Sharon, A. "What do adults read?" *Reading Research Quarterly,* 1973, *9,* 148-169.

Sticht, T.G. *Reading for working.* Alexandria, VA: Human Resources Research Organization, 1975.

Sticht, T.G. *Basic skills in defense.* Alexandria, VA: Human Resources Research Organization, 1982.

4
Occupational Literacy and Human Learning

During the past two decades, research has contributed much to the understanding of the processes of learning and memory in human beings. It may never be possible to describe exactly how these processes operate, but studies from the fields of cognitive psychology, computer science, and education suggest possible structures of memory and several factors which are involved in learning and remembering. This chapter provides a foundation for the instructional recommendations contained in Chapters 5 and 6. Here the discussion focuses on the structure and organization of human memory, the process of learning and memory, factors which affect learning and memory, and implications for literacy education and occupational training.

Understanding Learners

The Structure of Memory

Human memory is described in terms of three interactive component systems: immediate, short term, and long term. The efficiency with which any of the systems operates affects efficiency of the others.

Immediate memory, which is sometimes called perceptual trace (Travers, 1977) and described as a temporary sensory store, is very limited in both capacity and duration. An example of immediate memory in action (or inaction) can be taken from the daily experience of listening to the weather forecast. It is quite common for listeners to be aware of the broadcast without noting any of the key information. Similarly, most adults can recall the experience of having been introduced to a stranger, hearing the person's name, and forgetting it almost immediately.

Short term memory serves two important functions. First, it enables us to efficiently perform routine tasks requiring temporary storage of information. Second, short term memory enables us to store information in long term memory.

Short term memory is employed in tasks such as looking up and remembering a telephone number or remembering a list of tools and hardware which must be retrieved from one's basement or garage. Information is often rehearsed or organized in some way to facilitate retention in short term memory. Rehearsal of information is an effective means of facilitating memory for information over brief periods.

In cases where numbers or lists contain more than seven discrete items, reorganizing the items into smaller groups is known to be an effective means of enhancing short term memory. Telephone numbers and social security numbers are examples of long numbers which have been conveniently "chunked" for easy storage in short term memory.

It is also possible to organize nonnumeric information according to common characteristics. A long grocery list, for example, might be organized according to categories such as vegetables, meats, and dairy products. Similarly, such a list might be chunked according to the various aisles on which the items are located in a familiar grocery store. Organization of information in short term memory is critically important if that information is to be transferred to long term memory.

Long term memory was once thought to have unlimited capacity and duration; the existence of billions of cells in the human central nervous system suggested to many psychologists and educators that an equal number of bits of information could be stored. Reports of long forgotten memories being recalled in vivid detail as the result of surgical stimulation (Penfield, 1951) suggested that all experience was permanently stored in memory. Recent theory and research concerning human memory discount these once widely held beliefs. The capacity and duration of long term memory, though substantial, is limited and is affected by many factors, such as organization and practice.

Research suggests different models of the structure of long term memory, each dealing with the way in which information is organized to make efficient recall possible. Current models suggest that long term memory may be viewed as a system involving: 1) hierarchical classifications; 2) simplified base structure representations of ideas expressed through complex language (Kintsch & Keenan, 1973); or 3) as dual systems which process events and incidents differently from semantic information (Tulving, 1972). In each model, the central importance of organization is clear.

As a potential tool for educators, each model of long term memory merits discussion. The hierarchical classification model is familiar in that it is similar to the way in which school curricula are organized; dogs and cats are classified as mammals which are classified with fish and birds as animals. Organization involving categories and subcategories makes retrieval straightforward because the information has been stored in a predictable place in memory.

The model of memory which proposes that semantic information (typically emphasized in educational settings) is stored in a form simpler than the surface structure in which it is perceived is based on experiments such as those conducted by Kintsch (1974). These studies indicate that it takes longer to comprehend information presented in complex sentences than the same information presented in simple sentences. In either case, while the syntax is soon forgotten the basic information—the base structure—is remembered. Kintsch's term *proposition* denotes the base structure stored in memory. In propositional form, the sentences "The boy threw the ball" and "The ball was thrown by the boy" are represented by:

Throw: AGENT (boy), OBJECT (ball).

Tulving's dual system model of long term memory is based on evidence that incidents or episodes are stored differently from other forms of information. Episodic memory seems to be organized chronologically; events are stored in the order in which they occur. Semantic memory involves facts, formulas, and language oriented information which must be organized in some way before it can be stored in memory.

Information retrieved from episodic memory tends to be modified. Successive accounts of eye witness experiences, given by the same person, tend to differ. Knowledge such as facts, formulas, poems, or songs—the domain of semantic memory—tend to be unmodified in recall.

Episodic and semantic memory systems are parallel with iconic and symbolic memory categories posited by Piaget and Inhelder (1973). Iconic memory consists of images derived from perception, and iconic memories, like episodic memories, are prone to inaccuracy. Symbolic memories can be characterized as typically verbal and, like semantic memories, tend to be accurate and stable.

Factors Affecting Learning and Remembering

At least five factors are important to the processes of learning and memory: attention, meaning, involvement, organization, and practice.

Attention is the key factor in learning and remembering information from any source. Efficient learners pay attention. In listening, reading, or other activities they look for connections between their knowledge of the world and what they observe. An important characteristic of efficient learning and remembering is the use of prior knowledge and experience to guide and focus attention. Research by Kintsch and Keenan (1973) suggests that information stored in short term memory may be used to organize information for storage in long term memory.

Meaning implies that information, in order to be learned and remembered, must be personally meaningful to the learner. It is important for the learner to "see" how information to be learned is related to what is already known. Verbal or written instructions for the operation of a tractor are understandable only to the extent that the person hearing or reading the instructions is familiar with tractors or similar machines.

Involvement refers to the need for physical or mental manipulation of new information. Information which is consciously compared and contrasted with previously acquired knowledge is more effectively learned and remembered than information which is more passively processed. Involvement, in the form of mentally rewording information, is an effective way to personalize and thereby learn and remember.

Organization of information seems to be an important factor and function of short term memory. Indeed, a major function of short term memory seems to be the organizing of information for storage in long term memory (Kintsch, 1977). Through this process, effective learners arrange new information according to cues which allow it to be connected to prior knowledge and, thus, remembered and recalled. In order to better organize and store new information, the search for connections between new and old should be a conscious component of the learning and teaching processes.

Practice, or application, is a critical factor in tasks which demand that information be remembered. In short term memory, new information must be rehearsed if it is to be remembered even briefly. Long term memory for information depends on periodic review. When too much time elapses after the use of information stored in long term memory, the information is lost and must be obtained from sources other than memory.

Clearly, immediate short term and long term memory systems are interactive. Short term memory borrows information from long term storage and uses it to guide attention toward relevant information being processed by immediate memory. Appropriate information from immediate memory is then held in short term memory and, if the learning task demands, organized for storage in long term memory. Each phase of the process—attention, meaning, involvement, organization, and practice—affects learning and remembering. The three systems of memory and the factors involved in them interact in the processing of semantic information.

Learning and Remembering Semantic Information

Reading is a process which requires active mental involvement with the information presented. Effective readers pay careful attention to the meaning of the text they are reading. They actively involve themselves in connecting what they are reading with their existing knowledge and prior experience. They evaluate and interpret information as they read and either assimilate the information into their existing knowledge structures or, when the new information outweighs existing knowledge, accommodate the new information by modifying their knowledge structures (Pearson & Johnson, 1978).

In terms of their occurrence in daily work, activities involving reading account for substantial amounts of time. Results of the studies discussed in Chapters 2 and 3 indicate that workers are involved with tasks requiring work related reading for more than an hour each workday. Diehl and Mikulecky (1980) reported that workers in various occupational roles spend an average of 113 minutes per day reading.

Occupational training requires that students spend far more time reading than is spent by workers on the job. The average student in the training programs studied by the authors, spent approximately 3.4 hours per day reading occupationally related materials. This figure is probably a low estimate since only three courses from each of the full-time training programs were examined.

Reading tasks can be classified according to reader purposes. On the job, reading to obtain information for the accomplishment of work—reading-to-do (Sticht, 1975)—predominates. In educational settings, reading to acquire knowledge for later application—reading-to-learn—is most common. In neither setting, however, is reading-to-do nor reading-to-learn used exclusively.

Listening

It is not possible to discuss listening without also discussing understanding, learning, and memory. More than a passive perception of auditory stimuli, listening is a process which requires a listener's active mental involvement. Effective listening depends on careful attention, meaningful involvement and organization, and frequent summarization of information, as listeners reconstruct the meaning of what is heard in light of their existing knowledge and prior experience.

Research on listening suggests that language use requires listening 45 percent of the time in daily adult activity. Classroom lecture settings require students to listen approximately 70 percent of the time at the elementary school level and 90 percent of the time at the college level. Yet, school students in lecture settings may listen only about 30 percent of the time (Nichols & Stevens, 1957). Adults tend to forget 50 percent of lecture content within 24 hours of hearing it. Typically, 80 percent of information presented in lectures is forgotten after two weeks.

Listening tasks have been categorized as monitoring, information getting, and critical listening. Monitoring corresponds to immediate memory. Auditory information seemingly "goes in one ear and out the other" until some external or internal factor causes attention to be focused.

Listening to acquire information can be divided into tasks which require that information be obtained for immediate use, and tasks which require the learning of information for later use. Listening to instructions for completing a written examination is a listening-to-do task. Listening-to-learn involves tasks such as note taking during classroom lectures.

Critical listening deeply involves the listener with the information being presented. Evaluation of the speaker's motives and of the information presented are important aspects of critical listening. Emotional factors may influence the listening process during critical listening; because of the emotional impact of the speaker's presentation, listeners may be influenced to accept or reject the message.

Implications

Whether in traditional classroom and laboratory settings or in adult basic education or on-the-job training programs, instruction should consider current theory and knowledge of learning and the implications for reading and listening. Understanding, learning, and remembering information require active involvement of the learner in the process of linking new information with existing knowledge and prior experience.

The concept of comprehension as a process of constructing meaning from new and old information (Pearson & Johnson, 1978) has important implications for all educators. It is particularly important in occupational education where there are so many possibilities for concretely connecting the new and the old. Equipment, raw materials, and tools which can be used to help relate new information to existing knowledge and experience, are readily available in occupational and training environments.

Evidence of the structure and function of human memory suggests that instruction should be concerned with helping students to use their knowledge and experience to aid in the understanding and learning of new concepts and processes. It seems essential that teachers carefully consider the backgrounds of their students in preparing instruction, and include preview and review activities which call attention to the relationships between information learned earlier and that which is to be learned.

Instruction should also address the need for learner attention to the information which is to be learned. Motivation and interest are important to maintenance of attention so, whenever possible, teachers should use devices which help students to focus attention on relevant information. In occupationally related education, it may be enough to point out situations in which the information will be crucial, or how ignorance of the information might be dangerous or otherwise costly. In cases where the information cannot be readily related to work activities, teachers should at least indicate possible applications of the new information.

Meaningful involvement of the learner with new information is important to understanding and learning. When learners are actively engaged in relating new information to their personal experience, they tend to comprehend and remember it better than if they do not try to find such relationships.

Organization of information is an important consideration in the instructional process because research shows that clear, consistent organization of material to be learned aids both comprehension and memory. According to Bransford (1979), several factors seem important to good organization and comprehension. Clear expression of new concepts, main ideas, and relationships between ideas enhances understanding. Careful use of examples and nonexamples which represent important concepts is an important aspect of good organization which aids comprehension. Avoidance of irrelevant detail is valuable in the presentation of understandable information to learners. Finally, the language used to communicate new information should be syntactically simple; learners may be confused by sentence structures which are unfamiliar to them.

The conclusions of Irwin and Davis (1980) about comprehension and learning from text should be considered. They summarize several factors which contribute to the retention of written information: 1) information which is motivating and interesting is more easily understood and remembered than information which is unmotivating and dull; 2) student familiarity with the pattern of organization of a written text is a valuable aid to understanding and learning; 3) immediate and periodic reinforcement, or review, of learned information aids recall; 4) graphic and pictorial aids which support textual information can assist understanding and memory; 5) questions which focus on personal application of new concepts, ideas, and processes contribute positively to learning; and 6) student use of newly acquired information contributes to retention. The similarity of these conclusions to those of Rosenshine (1983) and Berliner (1981) about effective teaching suggests that such factors contribute to the learning of both written and auditory information.

The learning of information can be enhanced through the use of effective strategies for learning. Bransford (1979) notes that effective learners actively monitor their understanding of information and seek clarification when in doubt. They are better able to use their experience to evaluate and elaborate information. They can identify the potential significance of new information better than less able learners can. This is consistent with research by Mikulecky and Winchester (1983), who observe that superior workers in nursing occupations are better at thinking through tasks and applying appropriate reading and writing strategies, than are less proficient workers. Moreover, effective learners seem able to put new information into personally meaningful contexts. Theoretically, teachers who provide exposure to and practice in the use of self-monitoring strategies will have a positive effect on learning by teaching students *how* to learn.

Summary

This chapter discussed the structure of human memory, human learning, and factors important to those processes. A description of the structure of memory posited the existence of three systems: immediate, short term, and long term. In any task requiring understanding, learning, and remembering, the three systems of memory interact with one another. Key factors in learning and memory are attention, meaning, involvement, organization, and practice. These factors can be managed by presenters of information (teachers and writers), as well as by learners.

Comprehension and learning are viewed as processes in which learners must be actively involved in seeking connections between new information and that which they already know. In both reading and listening tasks, instruction should focus on the establishment of such connections.

References

Berliner, D. Academic learning time and reading achievement. In J.T. Guthrie (Ed.), *Comprehension and teaching: Research reviews.* Newark, DE: International Reading Association, 1981.

Bransford, J.D. *Human cognition: Learning, understanding, and remembering.* Belmont, CA: Wadsworth, 1979.

Diehl, W., and Mikulecky, L. The nature of reading at work. *Journal of Reading,* 1980, *24,* 221-227.

Irwin, J.W., and Davis, C. Assessing readability: The checklist approach. *Journal of Reading,* 1980, *24,* 124-130.

Kintsch, W. *The representation of meaning in memory.* Hillsdale, NJ: Erlbaum, 1974.

Kintsch, W. *Memory and cognition.* New York: John Wiley and Sons, 1977.

Kintsch, W., and Keenan, J.M. Reading rate and retention as a function of the number of propositions in the base structure of sentences. *Cognitive Psychology,* 1973, *5,* 257-274.

Mikulecky, L., and Winchester, D. Job literacy and job performance among nurses at varying employment levels. *Adult Education Quarterly,* 1983, *34,* 1-15.

Nichols, R., and Stevens, L. *Are you listening?* New York: McGraw-Hill, 1957.

Pearson, P.D., and Johnson, D.D. *Teaching reading comprehension.* New York: Holt, Rinehart and Winston, 1978.

Penfield, W. Memory mechanisms. *Transactions of the American Neurological Association,* 1951, *76,* 15-31.

Piaget, J., and Inhelder, B. *Memory and intelligence.* New York: Basic Books, 1973.

Rosenshine, B. Teaching functions in instructional programs. *Elementary School Journal,* 1983, *83,* 335-351.

Sticht, T.G. *Reading for working: A functional literarcy anthology.* Alexandria, VA: Human Resources Research Organization, 1975.

Travers, R.M.W. *Essentials of learning: An overview for students of education.* New York: Macmillan, 1977.

Tulving, E. Episodic and semantic memory. In E. Tulving and W. Donaldson (Eds.), *Organization and memory.* New York: Academic Press, 1972, 382-404.

5
Developing Occupational Literacy and Related Competencies

T he previous chapter discussed the structure of human memory and the nature of comprehension and learning. It was suggested that teachers and students can enhance the processes of comprehension and learning through careful attention, meaningful involvement with the information to be learned, and the use of organizational strategies to form personally meaningful links between new information and existing knowledge.

This chapter presents instructional strategies and techniques consistent with current theory and research concerning comprehension, learning, and memory. Major headings within the chapter identify key occupational literacy and linguistic competencies: reading, writing, and oral language. Beneath each major heading, aspects of instruction are presented for a general audience of educators who might contribute to the development of essential job related skills. Specific references are made to teaching at prevocational, vocational, adult basic, and on-the-job education levels.

Reading

In this section, a distinction is made between the reading skills necessary to meaningfully interpret visual information and the cognitive processes required to put that information to work or to learn and remember the information for later use.

Occupational literacy requires skill in learning from written materials as well as skill in reading to accomplish specific tasks. Reading-to-learn involves thoughtful, reflective mental processing of information so that it can be recalled and used long after it is read. Reading-to-learn generates "working knowledge"; it involves long term memory. Reading-to-do work involves following written instructions and finding information for immediate use. In reading-to-do tasks, information is remembered no longer than a few minutes, so short term memory skills are essential.

The purpose of the reading task differentiates reading-to-learn from reading-to-do. Comprehension on the job and in training involves the same skills: interpreting expository prose and graphics, relating printed information to existing equipment and materials, and interpreting technical vocabulary. Differences lie in the extent to which learning and memory are essential. On the job, learning through reading is seldom required. In fact, memorization is often discouraged by employers who stress the use of handbooks and checklists to improve accuracy in job performance.

Characteristics of Occupational Reading Materials

Regardless of the work or training environment in which they are found, occupational reading materials require competency in dealing with special visual and organizational factors. One important characteristic of occupational reading materials is the high frequency with which graphic aids (figures, diagrams, charts, tables, and pictures) appear. The use of tables to convey important information in a clear and economical way is extensive. Graphics occur in conjunction with and independent of textual information.

Second, written or printed instructions or directions to workers and students frequently appear in on-the-job and training program settings.

Third, work and training program tasks frequently call for workers or students to interpret handwritten or printed materials which refer to some object or tool with which they are working.

Fourth, each occupation presents a specialized vocabulary which workers/students must recognize and understand.

Finally, occupational reading materials employ expository styles of organizing information. Although written and printed materials range from tersely worded memoranda to highly complex technical documents, they are heavily laden with references to important technical operations, concepts, and relationships.

Educators at prevocational, vocational, adult basic, and on-the-job levels can account for each of the mentioned factors in their dealings with students and workers. The balance of this section focuses on methods of preparing students and workers for mastering reading related occupational competencies.

Reading-to-Do

Many of the reading skills relevant to this section are necessary in both reading to perform work and in reading to learning information. Skills which pertain to the characteristics of occupational reading materials in general are discussed first. The final part of this section deals with expository patterns of organization and the development of reading-to-learn competencies.

Graphic aids to comprehension which are typical of occupational reading materials include figures, diagrams, charts, graphs, pictures, and tables. Their purpose is to enhance reader comprehension of expository text. Since most readers ignore graphic aids when reading (which may reflect teacher admonitions in beginning reading experiences to "look at the words not the pictures"), formal instruction in how to interpret graphics seems necessary.

Methods of preparing readers to interpret effectively and use graphic aids in various school subjects are described by Sheperd (1978), Robinson (1978), and Singer and Donlan (1980). The recommendations which follow are applicable to occupational reading materials. References and examples from occupational settings are used as illustrations of how skills instruction can be applied to relevant materials.

Figures and diagrams are similar in that they usually take the form of drawings which illustrate textual information. Sticht (1980) notes that figures and diagrams often contain words which identify some aspect of the illustrated item. According to Robinson (1978), figures and diagrams are integral parts of explanations presented in accompanying written text. As such, they must be read in conjunction with the text through a series of back and forth referrals. A sound strategy for teaching learners to make good use of figures and diagrams is to train them to focus their attention on such graphic aids before examining the text itself. Learners should be encouraged to use a figure or diagram as a basis for preparing to read the accompanying text by setting purposes for reading. Just as readers can use headings and other print related cues as guides to more efficient reading, they can use figures, diagrams, and other graphic aids as cues for questions to be answered through careful reading.

The illustrations which follow show arrangements of textual information in conjunction with figures and diagrams. The examples are taken from occupationally related materials, but similar patterns are commonly found in classroom mathematics and science textbooks.

Example 1

Fixing a Leaking Faucet

Compression faucet. At the end of the stem of a compression faucet, is a washer held in place by a screw. When the faucet is turned off, the stem is screwed all the way down, and the washer fits snugly into the valve seat, stopping the flow of water. If the faucet is dripping from the end of the spigot, it is possible that either a washer or a valve seat has deteriorated.

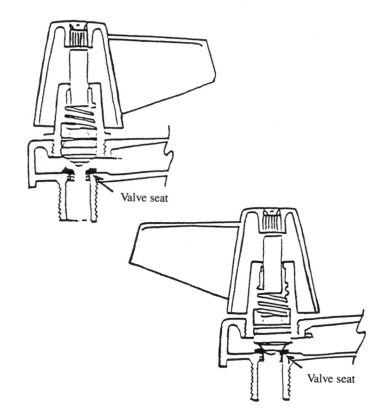

Top: Compression faucet is open. Bottom: Faucet is off, washer is compressed.

Charts show relationships between various components of an organization or process. Used frequently in the electronics and computer science industries, charts contribute clarifying concreteness by expressing complex information in visually simple formats. As with other forms of graphic aids, learners may not fully use charts unless they are taught to attend to and interpret them.

Instruction in the use of charts should be based on the understanding that these graphic aids are provided by writers because they summarize detailed information from the printed text. Learners should be instructed to recognize the purpose of the chart and then determine the organization of the chart, identify the meaning of the symbols used, and relate the chart to the accompanying text. Examples (see Example 2) might be employed to develop skill in using charts to full advantage in occupationally relevant reading tasks.

Example 2
TEXT WITH CHART

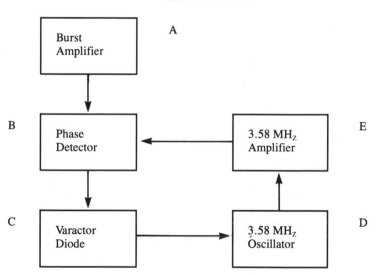

A. Amplifies the 3.58 MHz "burst" signal transmitted by the TV station. This signal is used as a reference for the demodulators to determine the beam intensity. The beam intensity, in turn, determines the proper amount of each color.

B. Compares the output frequency of the 3.58 MHz reference signal oscillator with the burst frequency, and generates a correction voltage.

C. Changes capacity as the correction voltage changes. This corrects the 3.58 MHz oscillator, making it the same frequency as the burst signal.

D. Creates a 3.58 MHz reference voltage; provides the reference to the demodulators to obtain correct color signals.

E. Amplifies the 3.58 MHz reference voltage for demodulators.

Graphs, like charts, summarize information which is presented in written or tabular form elsewhere. Three types of graphs predominate: bar (used to show differences in amount); line (used to show increases or decreases); and circle or pie (used to show proportional distributions of variables).

Guidelines for users of graphs should focus attention on the meaning of headings and labels, the comparison of information represented in the graph with textual information, and the evaluation of the relative importance of aspects of the graphically presented information.

Example 3 illustrates graphs found in occupational settings. In each case, the relevance of the information in the graph is determined by the text which acccompanies it.

Example 3
TEXT WITH GRAPH

Color, Automatic Color Control, and Color Killer Amplifiers

The video signal is coupled from the output of the IF circuit board through resistor R817 to pin 11 on the chroma circuit board. Coupling capacitator C353, coil L351, resistor R359, and capacitor C354 form a wave-shaping network at the 3.58 MH, color signal frequencies. The wave-shaping network passes the higher frequencies (color information) and limits the lower frequencies of the luminance signal.

Complete Television Signal for Channel 2

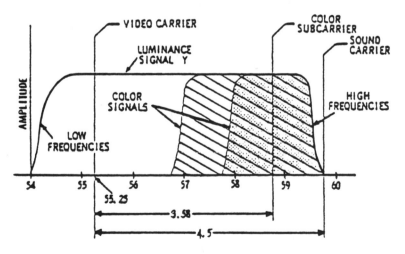

FREQUENCIES IN MEGAHERTZ

Occupational Literacy Education

Pictures are widely used in occupational settings and in occupational training. They often relate directly to a specific task, material, tool, or machine and are sometimes enhanced by arrows or circles which guide the user's attention. Because they establish a visual context which includes many environmental cues, pictures are useful and important aids to comprehension. Therefore, skill in the use of pictorial information is essential in occupational and training program settings.

Readers should learn to examine pictures as a prelude to reading for detail. The strategy of previewing and setting purposes before carefully reading the text should always include thoughtful examination of supplementary pictures. Example 4 shows combinations of pictures and accompanying text.

Example 4
TEXT AND PICTURE*

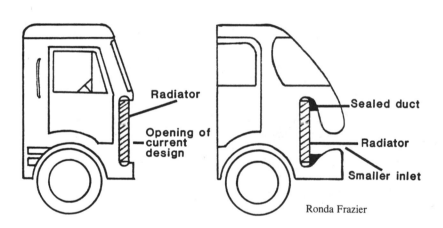

Ronda Frazier

Current truck radiator installation design (left) requires flat front. Air resistance can be reduced by a streamlined design (right) where ducts bring sufficient cooling air to the radiator.

* Through design improvement, over-the-road trucks can function with radiator openings one-third as large as those used currently. Sealing of ducts is necessary so that all cooling air is directed to the radiator. Applications of such truck designs have existed in the aircraft industry for many decades. Automotive engineers should examine aeronautical engineering practices in their quest for aerodynamic efficiency.

Tables often accompany graphs and are used to summarize numerical or statistical information. In interpreting tables, as in interpreting graphs, the user must attend to the general heading of the table as well as to the headings of its rows and columns of numbers. Tabular information must then be compared and interpreted in light of the textual information it accompanies. In Example 5, the reader must associate the information in the table with the task at hand and with the information provided in text.

Example 5

TEXT AND TABLE

Low Hydrogen Electrodes

Hydrogen has harmful effects on alloy steels, causing intergranular cracks called hydrogen embrittlement thus lowering fatigue resistance and strength.

RIGHT HAND DIGIT	COVERING COMPOSITIONS	APPLICATION (USE)
5 E-7015	Low hydrogen sodium type.	This is a low hydrogen electrode for welding low carbon, alloy steels. Power shovels and other earth moving machinery require this rod. The weld machines or files easily. Use DC, RP only.
6 E-7016	Same as 5 but with potassium salts used for arc stabilizing.	It has the same general application as 5 above except it can be used on either DC, RP, or AC.
E-7027	High iron oxide (Low Hydrogen). Flat and horizontal fillet weld position.	For low carbon alloy steels, use DC or AC.
E-7028	Iron powder (Low Hydrogen). Flat position only.	For low carbon alloy steels, use DC or AC.
8 E-8018	Iron powder plus low hydrogen sodium covering.	Similar to 5 and 6, DC, RP, or AC. Heavy covering allows the use of high speed drag welding. AC or DC RP may be used.

Low hydrogen electrode covering Compositions and Applications. These coverings will withstand a high temperature and therefore high currents (amperages) may be used.

Following instructions involves the ability to read and carry out written or printed instructions. It is an essential skill which requires methodical reading and intense concentration. When teaching learners how to follow written instructions, it is best to emphasize that such reading is hard work and requires a slow, careful approach.

Occupational Literacy Education

The process of reading and following instructions parallels the reflective process of the Directed Reading-Thinking Activity (DRTA, described under reading-to-learn) and similar approaches to reading for learning and studying purposes. In reading to follow instructions and reading-to-learn, readers are required to be aware of their purposes, to demonstrate their comprehension, and to evaluate their interpretation of what they have read. The essential difference lies in the application of skills. In most situations, DRTA and similar methods are applied to chapter length segments of text; following instructions usually involves brief passages. Unlike reading to follow instructions, reading-to-learn from text seldom requires an immediate physical response from readers.

Instruction in reading and following instructions should include cautionary statements about the need for care and concentration. Also, practice should be required in applying a systematic, self-directed approach to samples of written instructions. Specific rules might be stated in this way:

1. Develop a mental set for what is to be done by reading the instructions once completely.
2. Read the first step carefully and do as it directs.
3. Reread the step and check your work.
4. Read, do, and reread each of the remaining steps until all are accomplished.
5. Reread and check your work for the whole set of instructions.

In most classrooms, a variety of materials is available for use in teaching learners to carry out instructions. Written instructions for daily assignments can provide frequent practice when used to full advantage by teachers. Such instructions, however, require careful attention from teachers. Poorly prepared instructions may cause frustration and discourage independent action by learners. The effect of carefully prepared instructions can be subverted by teachers who consistently repeat or restate classroom instructions since attention to instructions is unnecessary when repetitions are readily available.

A method of stressing attention to instructions is to provide written instructions, for which no supplemental help is available, for at least one activity per day. As learners develop skill with written instructions, the number of daily assignments can be increased.

The use of sets of instructions closely related to those encountered in the workplace is an important teaching consideration. Laboratory activities from biological, physical, and social science curricula are good sources of instructions. Mathematics textbooks may include many well-prepared problems which require careful reading. Educational games, model building kits, recipes, and instructions for household appliances are also good sources of material for extending practice of an important skill into the "real world."

Occupational and training tasks often require readers to interpret and integrate printed, graphic, and physical information to materials, tools, and equipment.

As in the case of instructions involving written language alone, it is important that learners understand the importance of slow, methodical reading and complete concentration when following instructions. This is especially true in tasks which combine written, graphic, and physical information. Given this understanding, rules can be taught for reading instructions which involve existing materials.

A set of guidelines, derived from a student self-evaluation checklist for science laboratory reading (Thomas & Robinson, 1977), is relevant to the many tasks which require reading to guide the manipulation of materials, tools, and equipment.

1. Skim the instructions to establish a mind set. Note titles, headings, and graphic aids, and read the introduction and study questions.
2. Familiarize yourself with any materials or equipment involved in the task.
3. Read the entire procedure.
4. Verify the meanings of words and symbols of which you are unsure.
5. Read and do each step with great concentration, paying special attention to difficult or unclear steps. These should be reread and thoughtfully interpreted.
6. Read numeric information with exactness.
7. Pay special attention to cautionary words such as *danger, caution, note,* and *attention.*
8. Make use of graphic aids by consciously relating them to both the text and equipment at hand.
9. Be alert to the order/sequence in which steps are to be done.
10. Reflect on what you are doing while you are working.
11. After completing the procedures, carefully evaluate what you have done in light of the instructions. Using a written or mental checklist, check off each completed step in sequence.

Learners should be made aware that concentrated effort is necessary to gain an understanding of the function or operation of materials, tools, and equipment.

Guidelines for such tasks should require that learners take active roles in planning controlled reading. First, headings, pictures, graphs, introductions, and summaries are surveyed to establish a mental set for subsequent careful reading. Next, purposes are set for reading small sections of the text. Careful reading follows with purposes in mind. Frequent back and forth references between print, graphics, and physical media are made to verify understanding. Then, in their own words, readers attempt to develop a brief explanation of what has been read. If only poor explanations can be stated, readers must reread to find the causes of the gaps in understanding. This procedure is similar to several procedures for effective reading and study, including the Directed Reading-Thinking Activity (Stauffer, 1980), which is described in the reading-to-learn section.

Reading-to-Assess

Students should work with reading materials and tasks directly related to those actually found in occupational settings. Whenever possible, reading materials should be used in worklike activities (Sticht, 1982). Reading-to-do tasks, involving finding and using information, should be addressed as essential occupational skills.

Analysis of *whether, when,* and *how* to use reading materials is a crucial occupational reading skill. Like skills in finding and using information, reading-to-assess skills can be practiced through teacher developed work simulations (Mikulecky & Winchester, 1983).

A work simulation might involve correctly setting an electronic wristwatch. At a classroom center, learners would be required to select the appropriate reference from among technical textbooks, electrical handbooks, and sets of instructions for several electrical appliances.

Reading-to-Learn

The reading skills discussed in the previous section are as important in tasks requiring learning through reading as they are in tasks which require the accomplishment of work. With respect to learning, however, there are key aspects of reading which are more important than in reading-to-do tasks. These include the systematic approach to reading for study purposes and skill in interpreting information which is presented in the various organizational patterns used by writers of expository prose.

An orientation to the reading-to-learn process is acquired indirectly through most developmental reading programs. Such programs systematically prepare readers to make mental connections between their existing knowledge and the information they read. Approaches such as the DRTA are typical of developmental reading programs and involve the following steps or stages:

1. Previewing the material to establish a mind set for reading.
2. Setting purposes for reading by using headings, subheadings, and graphic aids as sources of questions to be answered.
3. Careful reading with purposes in mind.
4. Recitation—formulation of answers to questions or relating key information to prior knowledge. (These are always personalized responses in the reader's own words.)
5. Rereading as necessary to find answers to questions formulated in step 2 or to clarify relationships between the new information and prior knowledge.

Directed reading activities are effective tools in reading-to-learn because, through the process of rewording key information, learners are required to associate important ideas, concepts, and relationships with their prior knowledge. The recitation component usually involves the association of new information with prior knowledge through personally meaningful examples. Further, recitation serves as a method of self-monitoring comprehension; key points cannot be restated if they have not been recognized and understood.

Most approaches to developmental reading emphasize strategies necessary in reading-to-learn. Teachers can stress the relevance of such strategies in the world of work by planning lessons which highlight work related applications of reading. Frequent use of exercises involving occupationally relevant materials could enhance the practical value of preoccupational and occupational courses.

Essential organizational differences exist between narrative and expository prose. Narrative prose is typically organized according to a plot, or story grammar. Readers become familiar with narrative patterns through listening and reading experiences. Expository prose can be organized in one of several patterns which, because of their infrequent use in literature, require formal instructional attention.

The skills required for reading expository materials may be taught through early and frequent experiences with written materials which impart factual or technical information. Prevocational level social studies, science, mathematics, and developmental reading textbooks are good sources of such material. Tradebook authors such as Roy Gallant and Isaac Asimov have published many short, readable books explaining subjects of interest to upper elementary and secondary school readers. Such books can be useful in developing skill in reading expository prose in its various organizational forms.

Social studies materials are written in styles also common in occupational reading materials. Patterns such as contextual definitions, enumeration of examples, classification of information, sequences of steps and stages, comparison and contrast, and cause and effect frequently appear in both social studies and work related contexts. Robinson (1978) presents detailed descriptions of these organizational patterns and their implications for instruction. Although his discussion focuses on social studies, it is quite relevant reading for those whose instructional concerns are related to other technical subjects. It is possible and appropriate for expository reading skills to be introduced in elementary school social studies and applied and practiced at each grade level through formal occupational training.

Prevocational classroom science and mathematics programs also employ patterns of organization which occur frequently in work related written materials. Common patterns include enumeration, sequence, comparison and contrast, cause and effect, and if/then relationships. Instruction in reading such patterns may begin in the early grades and continue for the duration of formal education.

Early and repeated experiences with materials written in expository style will enable learners and workers to focus their attention on key information without becoming confused by unfamiliar writing styles. Also, the importance of listening to expository prose being read correctly should be emphasized. For example, oral reading of difficult or unfamiliar material by an instructor who understands how punctuation affects phrasing provides learners with models to apply in independent reading. Teachers should encourage learners to read complex or difficult materials aloud as a means of aiding comprehension.

General recommendations concerning learning through reading include the use of an approach such as the DRTA in planned sessions involving short periods of intensive study interspersed with brief intervals of unrelated activity. Authorities recommend twenty minute periods of study in college level skills development. Long periods of cramming have little effect on long term retention of information and should be avoided. Learning through reading is much more effective when knowledge is gradually acquired and periodically reviewed.

In higher level prevocational courses and vocational education, students should focus on their long range goal, the acquisition of working knowledge, rather than on short term goals of merely "passing the test." Such a focus makes it more likely that learners will carefully plan study time and use appropriate techniques of reading and study.

Writing

A review of the third chapter shows that writing in skilled and semi-skilled occupations does not require a high level of sophistication. With the exception of the secretarial occupation, standard usage is less important than clarity of communication. Handwriting styles vary considerably, even in the drafting occupation. Hence clarity, as exemplified by legibility, is again the critical factor but a wide range of legible styles is accepted.

Clarity of written expression and handwriting seems to be of greater importance than standard usage in occupational communication. Thus, instruction in job related writing skills should focus on clear communication of information. A telegraphic style of writing, clear and concise, might be used to develop initial skills:

Smith,

    Attach return hydraulic hose to frontloader. See me.

                                                                Jones

Messages such as this also could be used as a basis for instruction in standard forms of English usage. Exercises might require the combining of telegraphic phrases and sentences into more complex, fluent sentences.

Oral Language

Listening effectively is a crucial competency in work and training program environments. As in the case of reading, listening is used both to facilitate the accomplishment of work tasks and to enable the learning of information for later use. The purpose of the listening task determines the relative importance of short and long term memory. In either application of listening, similar skills are required.

The key skill in effective listening is actively focused attention. No matter what the situation, if the listener fails to focus on the message given by the speaker, no information is comprehended. Teachers need to demonstrate ways for learners to improve the ability to pay close attention during listening activities. One approach is to demonstrate the consequences of inattentive listening. Safety films, speakers from local businesses, and classroom activities which require learners to follow aural instructions or to relate personal experiences in which poor listening caused problems are methods of focusing on the need for improvement.

There are several causes of poor listening; most involve inattention. Comprehension of information is reduced when listeners allow their minds to wander, allow themselves to respond emotionally to the speaker, are distracted by environmental factors, are distracted by annoying characteristics of the speaker, listen for detail rather than for central ideas, or are reluctant to work at listening.

In both listening-to-do work and listening-to-learn, the following guidelines can lead to more efficient processing information.

1. Use what you already know about the speaker's subject to help you listen and learn.
2. Try to anticipate what the speaker will say next.
3. Listen for main ideas and relationships between them.
4. Make frequent summaries of main ideas and relationships in your own words.
5. Monitor your comprehension of what is being said and think about it.
6. Ask questions when you are not sure that you understand.

In addition to these general guidelines, awareness of certain aspects of occupational settings might be stressed. In most job related situations, there are environmental factors which can be used to enhance listening. Speakers frequently refer to objects close at hand. Sketches are often employed to clarify the meaning of what is said. Rarely are instructions given outside a specific and familiar context. Thus, if listeners alert themselves to the available clues in the occupational settings, they will be better able to cope with the listening demands of those settings. Newcomers to a job or training program should be particularly attentive to available clues to listening. As they become familiar with people and equipment in their new surroundings, attention to relevant clues will become second nature.

Speaking

Clarity of communication is essential in occupational settings; however, leeway in levels of grammar and usage is granted in most situations. A short, clear, grammatically imperfect message is much preferred to a misleading, grammatically perfect one.

Perhaps the best advice to speakers in occupationally related settings is to focus on making sure the message is clearly understood by the listener. Several precautions can be taken to assure clear communication.

1. Prepare your listeners by helping them associate what you are going to say with what they already know. Tell them how the instructions you are giving are related to what you asked them to do yesterday. Establish a context for your information.

2. Use environmental clues to aid your listeners in attending and understanding. Equipment, pictures, and diagrams enhance listening and understanding.
3. Be attentive to nonverbal and verbal signs of inattention and/or confusion on the part of your listeners. Listener responses such as "uh-huh" or "yes" are not evidence of attention or understanding, especially when accompanied by vacant or puzzled facial expressions.
4. When your listeners seem inattentive and confused, restate your message in different terms.
5. Observe yourself as you give information or instructions. Be alert to actions or mannerisms which might be distracting or misleading.
6. Be clear in your use of context and environmental cues.

Fortunately for speakers, oral language allows for reinforcement of information so that miscommunication need not occur. The trick is to focus on making sure the message is clear and that listeners are receiving it.

Summary

This chapter has reviewed the nature of reading, writing, and oral language requirements in occupational settings and described some instructional approaches to provide learners with occupational literacy and related competencies.

Mikulecky's research (1982) shows that workers consistently read more diverse materials, in greater depth, for more times per day, and with greater purpose than do secondary students. Workers also view reading as more important than do students. These findings have important implications for teachers at all levels. Instructional attention must be given to reading-to-do skills, to finding and applying information which is presented in graphic form, and to following written instructions.

The required competencies are much less complex in writing and oral language than in reading. The focus of successful performance in these occupational literacy related areas is on clarity of communication. Learners in school settings should strive for mastery of standard English usage, but they should also become familiar with the telegraphic, nonstandard styles in which much occupational communication occurs.

In all instructional matters, a healthy concept for teachers to bear in mind is that knowledge and skills need application if effective learning is to take place. By applying skills to occupational examples, two purposes may be simultaneously met: 1) Enhanced retention of knowledge and skills through realistic practice, and 2) genuine appreciation of the value of such knowledge and skills. It seems worth the effort to connect the school to the workplace.

References

Mikulecky, L. Job literacy: The relationship between school preparation and workplace actuality. *Reading Research Quarterly,* 1982, *17,* 400-419.

Mikulecky, L., and Winchester, D. Job literacy and job performance among nurses at varying employment levels. *Adult Education Quarterly,* 1983, *34,* 1-15.

Robinson, H.A. *Teaching reading and study strategies: The content areas,* second edition. Boston: Allyn and Bacon, 1978.

Sheperd, D.L. *Comprehensive high school reading methods,* second edition. Columbus, OH: Charles E. Merrill, 1978.

Singer, H., and Donlan, B. *Reading and learning from text.* Boston: Little-Brown, 1980.

Solid state color television model GR-269. Benton Harbor, MI: Heath, 1971.

Stauffer, R.G. *The language experience approach to the teaching of reading,* second edition. New York: Harper and Row, 1980.

Sticht, T.G. Minimum competency in functional literacy for work. In R.M. Jaeger and C.K. Tittle (Eds.), *Minimum competency achievement testing.* Berkeley, CA: McCutchan, 1980.

Sticht, T.G. *Basic skills in defense.* Alexandria, VA: Human Resources Research Organization, 1982.

Thomas, E.L., and Robinson, H.A. *Improving reading in every class.* Boston: Allyn and Bacon, 1972.

6

Technical Vocabulary Development

T eachers must focus on the essential knowledge and skills of their subjects. Reading and literacy related skills, critical to comprehension and learning, are part of the essential content of every subject. Yet it is doubtful that many teachers devote much time to direct instruction in such skills.

Mikulecky's research (1982) suggests the importance of increasing teacher awareness of subject related reading competencies. He found differences in the quality and quantity of reading in school compared to reading on the job, and observed that the reading demands placed on workers exceed those experienced by high school students. For example: 1) on-the-job reading requires more time per day than in-school reading; 2) workers read a wider variety of materials for more specific purposes than do high school students; 3) compared to technical school students, workers see reading as more important to success; and 4) workers do significantly more applications oriented reading.

If, as this evidence suggests, reading and related skills merit instructional attention before and during occupational training, a logical place to start is with the teaching of essential vocabulary. Each occupation has its particular set of requirements which include literacy and language competencies. Each has a specialized vocabulary essential to understanding, learning, and communication. The words which make up the technical vocabulary of a subject or occupation fit two categories: 1) True technical words, which seldom occur in normal usage (i.e., *suprarenal, syndrome, hypotenuse,* and *heliarc*), and 2) multiple meaning words, everyday words with special meanings (i.e., *field, root, leg, branch, strike, plug,* and *tape*).

In light of the strong relationship between word knowledge and comprehension (Davis, 1944, 1968; Spearitt, 1972) and learning (Anderson & Freebody, 1979), the need is clear for systematic instruction which emphasizes meaningful application of knowledge and skills. Such instruction should enable learners to independently determine the meanings of unfamiliar words.

Awareness of Words

A comprehensive program of vocabulary development should create a general awareness of words and their relationships as a prerequisite to instruction in specific vocabulary skills. Such an awareness can be fostered through methods described by Johnson and Pearson (1984) and Johnson (1984). Their instructional recommendations stress the need for connecting words to the various contexts in which they might occur. Several related methods are appropriate for accomplishing such instruction.

A method of showing connections between words and contexts, known as semantic webbing or mapping, seems particular valuable in specialized and occupational studies. The basic procedure for constructing a semantic map involves 1) selecting a key word, 2) brainstorming as many related words as possible, 3) categorizing the related words, 4) preparing a diagram which shows word relationships, and 5) optionally selecting a word from the map to serve as the core of a new map.

Example 1 shows a possible semantic map of the word *pressure.* Maps such as this are useful because they graphically illustrate the relationships between words and the differing shades of meaning which they take on in different settings.

Semantic mapping can be modified to emphasize the value of learning word parts—prefixes, suffixes, and roots. Example 2 presents a map of the Latin prefix *trans* (across).

Maps of word parts illustrate the relationships between similar words. Also, maps graphically present the power of mastery over word parts; knowing the meaning of *trans* unlocks virtually scores of words for the reader.

Semantic feature analysis is a second method of orienting learners toward words and word relationships. Like semantic mapping, this method requires learners to use their knowledge and experience to expand their vocabulary. Use of semantic feature analysis requires these basic steps: 1) selecting a category or topic, 2) identifying terms to list beneath the category, 3) listing features in a row beside the category, and 4) marking correspondences between words and features.

Example 3 shows a semantic feature chart for the category, *tools.*

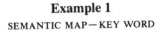

Example 1
SEMANTIC MAP—KEY WORD

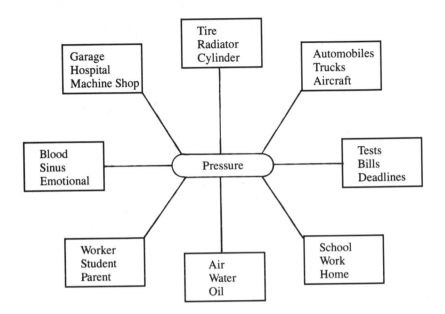

	Tire Radiator Cylinder	
Garage Hospital Machine Shop		Automobiles Trucks Aircraft
Blood Sinus Emotional	Pressure	Tests Bills Deadlines
Worker Student Parent	Air Water Oil	School Work Home

Example 2
SEMANTIC MAP—WORD PART

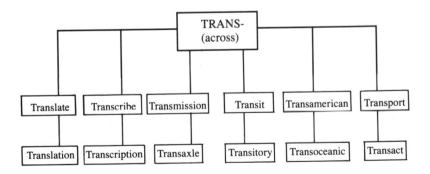

TRANS-
(across)

Translate	Transcribe	Transmission	Transit	Transamerican	Transport
Translation	Transcription	Transaxle	Transitory	Transoceanic	Transact

Example 3

SEMANTIC FEATURE ANALYSIS

TOOLS

FEATURES

Terms	Measure	Adjust	Cut	Cars	Build
Pliers		x		x	x
Tape	x				x
Caliper	x	x		x	x
Screwdriver				x	x
File			x	x	x

After awareness of words and word relationships has been developed through the foregoing methods, independent vocabulary skills can be taught. Training in specific vocabulary skills can be based on the recommendations of Deighton (1959), who described the importance of context clues, word analysis, dictionary and glossary use, and other text based aids.

Context Clues

Learners and workers should be made aware that context clues are efficient and powerful tools for determining the meanings of unfamiliar words. In most situations, readers can apply their knowledge of the context surrounding an unfamiliar word to determine its meaning. Teachers and learners should be aware, however, that context clues are not foolproof. Context at best reveals only a single meaning and frequently provides only partial meaning. Context contributes to vocabulary growth in proportion to the amount of reading done. In general, reliance on context alone yields very gradual vocabulary growth.

Context clues may be more effective in specialized subjects and occupational settings in which expository materials are prevalent. Writers of technically oriented textbooks and reference materials commonly employ devices which increase the value of context in determining word meaning. *Definition, example,* and *restatement* are three frequently used literary devices which clarify the meanings of key words in technical writing. In fact, Deighton (1959) recommended these devices to writers as means of enhancing the value of context as a tool for vocabulary development.

An instance of the use of *definition* follows:

Flashing is then installed. Flashing is sheet metal installed around the base of the chimney so that water is prevented from running under the roofing material.

Here, the writer has deliberately provided a clear definition of the term immediately after its introduction.

Example is very often used in technical writing to clarify new words.

Orienting skills, *especially* map reading and compass use, are essential to the wilderness hiker.

In this case, the writer has used the word *especially* to signal the reader that a clarifying example is about to be presented. Other words which signal examples include *such as, for example,* and *for instance.*

Restatement may not be as clearly connected to the unfamiliar word as definition or example, but awareness of this device can be an asset to readers of technical materials. In the following sentence, the writer has presented the meaning of the new word without using a separate sentence or a signal word.

The technician sometimes makes a *hypothesis,* an educated guess, about the cause of a malfunction.

The term *hypothesis* has been restated in more familiar words.

Word Analysis

A second major component of a program of technical vocabulary development is word analysis. Its use requires knowledge of word parts and their meanings—prefixes, suffixes, and word roots. There is some disagreement about the amount of emphasis the study of word parts should receive, but in specialized fields such study seems appropriate. High frequency word parts with consistent meanings should be considered part of the content of specialized and occupational studies.

Lists of word parts which have utility in general education can be found in Thomas and Robinson (1977), Sheperd (1978), and Deighton (1959). Examination of the vocabulary of work, presented in the appendices, suggests that the following prefixes and suffices should be taught in occupationally oriented programs.

Prefixes

a, ab (away from)
ad (to, toward)
com, con (with)
de (from)
dis (apart, not)
en (in)
ex (out)
im, in (in, into)

non (not)
ob (against)
pre, pro (before)
re (back)
sub (under)
trans (across)
un (not)

Number prefixes

uni, mono (one)
du, bi (two)
tri (three)
quad, tetra (four)
quin, pent (five)
sex, hex (six)
sept (seven)
oct (eight)

dec (ten)
cent, hect (hundred)
mill, kilo (hundred)
semi, dcmi, hemi (half)
mega (million)

Suffixes

able, ible
age
al
ance
ant
ate
ble
ent

er, or
ing
ity
ly
or
sion
ship
tion

Roots derived from Latin and Greek which have occupational applications

acqu, hydra (water)
aud (hear)
auto (self)
bio (life)
duct (lead)
equ (equal)
fract, rupt (break)
geo (earth)
mag, magni (great)
man, manu (hand)
meter (measure)

mis, mit (send)
mov, mot (move)
par (get ready)
pli (fold)
part (carry)
sta, stat (stand)
spect, spic (see)
string, strict (tighten)
tract (draw, drag)
vid, vis (see)

Graphic aids

In addition to context and word analysis, another text related factor — graphic aids — contributes to vocabulary development. A previous chapter presented procedures for teaching learners how to take advantage of graphs, tables, figures, and pictures to aid comprehension. Example 4 illustrates the value of graphics in defining key words.

Context clues, word analysis, and graphic aids, used alone or in concert, enable readers to determine word meanings effectively and efficiently. In work and training settings, it is sometimes necessary to know complete and precise definitions of key words. Thus, skill in using glossaries and dictionaries is important to both workers and students.

Glossaries are included in many textbooks and reference materials found in occupational settings. Although glossaries provide the precise meaning intended by the writer, they are frequently overlooked by the readers. Readers should recognize that while most glossaries appear as appendices to entire books, writers frequently place glossaries in chapters or in page margins near the first occurrences of key words. Margin glosses are shown in Example 5. Note the proximity of the glosses to the words they define.

Dictionaries are often the last resort in the search for word meaning because, like glossaries, their use requires interruption of the reading act. Nevertheless, the ability to use dictionaries is important because they may be the only sources of knowledge about word pronunciation and precise meaning. Dictionaries also reinforce the importance of context; they require readers to choose from several definitions the one which best fits the context in which the unfamiliar word has occurred.

To Elementary Educators

Thus far, this chapter has dealt with recommendations to instructors of specialized and occupationally related subjects. There is much that can be done at earlier stages of the educational process to inspire interest in and awareness of words. The intensity of focus will vary according to the grade level of the learners, but teachers should be sensitive to opportunities to connect words, word parts, and vocabulary skills with the world of work.

The strategy of connecting vocabulary with occupational applications can be employed early in the educational experience. Many words which have special meanings in work settings are introduced in elementary school

Example 4
GRAPHIC DEFINITION

TOOLS

SCREWDRIVERS

Square blade shank can take wrench

Standard blade and tip for general use

Stubby screwdriver for tight spots

WRENCHES

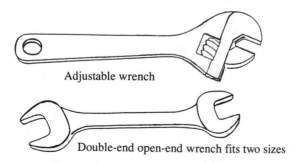

Adjustable wrench

Double-end open-end wrench fits two sizes

Example 5
MARGIN GLOSSES

Typing Text

The cursor shows where something will happen next.

The display should be blank, except for the blinking *cursor* and a row of letters and numbers across the top called the *Data Line*. The Data Line is important to many of Apple Writer's commands and capabilities, as you will see later. Before we learn about the Data Line, though, let's learn the basics. You bought Apple Writer because you wanted to type documents, so let's type.

In Apple Writer words automatically wrap around to the next line. Word wraparound means automatic carriage return.

Did you notice the display when the cursor moved to the end of the line? When there wasn't enough room for a word at the end of the line, the cursor took the word and automatically moved it down to the beginning of the next line. It's an automatic carriage return, commonly referred to as *word wraparound*.

Keep typing (type anything you want) until you feel comfortable with the idea of not pressing RETURN at the end of each line.

From AppleWriter II for IIe only. Permission granted by Apple Computer, Inc.

subjects. Teachers should routinely remark about the work meanings of such words.

Many of the prefixes, suffixes, and roots listed occur in primary grade reading materials. Words in which these parts appear can be readily associated with words from technical fields.

Field trips to school laboratories, shops, kitchens, nurses' offices, and administrative offices can help promote vocabulary awareness and growth when materials and equipment are labeled. Similarly, key words can be taught prior to and reviewed after class outings.

The recommendations of this chapter are not exhaustive. Teachers who wish to strengthen their vocabulary development programs should read the references cited. Works by Dale, O'Rourke, and Bamman (1971) and Johnson and Pearson (1984) should be of particular value at the elementary school level.

Occupational Literacy Education

Summary

This chapter, suggesting that few teachers deal effectively with technical vocabulary, has presented methods and information for vocabulary development. In any situation in which reading and word knowledge are important to human performance, formal instruction in vocabulary development is necessary and relatively easy to provide. Instructional methods from several sources have been recommended. Especially useful are those described by Johnson and Pearson because such methods as semantic mapping and semantic feature analysis are both excellent and appropriate for those who teach children or adults.

Instructional techniques have been described, but methods and materials are only part of vocabulary development. Teacher awareness of the close relationship between word knowledge and comprehension may be the essential element in bringing technical vocabulary instruction into every classroom.

References

Anderson, R.C., and Freebody, P. *Vocabulary Knowledge and learning.* Reading Education Report No. 11, University of Illinois at Urbana-Champaign, 1979.

Apple writer II: For e only. Cupertino, CA: Apple Computer, 1982.

Dale, E., O'Rourke, J., and Bamman, H.A. *Techniques of teaching vocabulary.* Menlo Park, CA: Benjamin/Cummings Publishing, 1971.

Davis, F.B. Fundamental factors of comprehension in reading. *Psychometrika,* 1944, *9,* 185-197.

Davis, F.B. Research in comprehension in reading. *Reading Research Quarterly,* 1968, *3,* 499-545.

Deighton, L.C. *Vocabulary development in the classroom.* New York: Bureau of Publications, Teachers College, Columbia University, 1959.

Johnson, D.D. Expanding vocabulary through classification. In J.F. Baumann and D.D. Johnson (Eds.), *Reading instruction for beginning teachers: A practical guide.* Minneapolis, MN: Burgess, 1984.

Johnson, D.D., and Pearson, P.D. *Teaching reading vocabulary,* second edition. New York: Holt, Rinehart and Winston, 1984.

Mikulecky, L. Job literacy: The relationship between school preparation and workplace actuality. *Reading Research Quarterly,* 1982, *17,* 400-419.

Sheperd, D.L. *Comprehensive high school reading methods,* second edition. Columbus, OH: Charles E. Merrill, 1978.

Spearitt, D. Identification of subskills of reading comprehension by maximum likelihood factor analysis. *Reading Research Quarterly,* 1972, *8,* 92-111.

Thomas, E.L., and Robinson, H.A. *Improving reading in every class: A source-book for teachers,* second edition. Boston: Allyn and Bacon, 1977.

Occupational Literacy Education

Appendix A
Highest Frequency Words
for Ten Occupations

The following list shows the 100 words most frequently used by adults in a study of ten skilled and semiskilled occupations and related training programs. The list is based on combined samples of written and oral language from all job and training program sites. The words comprise 45 percent of all language sampled.

Total Words = 180,000
Unique Words = 9,000

the	will	your	see
of	one	was	more
to	not	get	these
and	an	has	into
a	there	must	just
is	can	any	them
in	when	he	down
it	out	got	time
for	we	know	about
that	which	them	been
you	what	don't	some
be	do	each	business
or	up	air	how
on	pressure	check	its
are	two	that's	back
I	so	but	over
this	they	system	work
with	here	through	would
as	other	valve	temperature
by	okay	going	same
if	right	well	also
have	no	use	where
all	used	than	now
at	may	it's	only
from	should	go	like

Appendix B
Technical Vocabulary Lists

T his section contains two vocabulary lists derived from written and oral language samples from each of ten occupations. For each occupation, a brief list of high frequency technical words precedes a complete technical vocabulary.

Common words from everyday adult language (found in the most frequent 1,000 words of the Kucera-Francis list, *Computational analysis of present day American English,* Brown University Press, 1967) have been deleted from the technical vocabulary lists. Also removed are numerals; labels; names of people, places, products, and companies; contractions and possessives; and colloquialisms.

Some of the words in the lists are uncommon words which may not be technical in nature. The lists should, therefore, be treated as sources rather than standards. In each technical vocabulary list, the most frequent words are marked with asterisks.

The following table shows the total number of words and the number of unique words contained in the original language sample for each occupation.

VOCABULARY DATA

Occupation	Total Sample Words	Unique Words
Account Clerk	20,055	2,981
Auto Mechanic	20,900	3,034
Draftsman	27,874	3,414
Electrician	20,492	3,126
Heating/Air Conditioning Mechanic	19,937	2,841
Industrial Maintenance Mechanic	21,000	3,164
Licensed Practical Nurse	24,964	3,955
Machine Tool Operator	15,200	2,473
Secretary	15,259	2,492
Welder	13,687	2,375

HIGH FREQUENCY WORDS
ACCOUNT CLERK

accountant
accounting
accounts
actual
add
annual
application
appropriate
assets
balance
bank
businesses
capital
cash
check(s)
computes
contract
corporate
corporation
credit
date

debts
depreciating
depreciation
dollars
eight
employees
exempt(ion)
expense(s)
fees
fifty
file
fund(s)
gross
inventory
investment
item
joint
legal
liability
liable

maintains
monthly
net
nine
offer
organization
owners
partially
partner(s)
partnership
payment(s)
payroll
percent(age)
prepares
principal
profit
proprietor
purchase(d)
purposes
quarterly

reasonable
receipts
receives
related
reports
request(s)
revenue(s)
sale
sell(ing)
separate
shares
sheet
sold
statements
stockholders
taxable
taxes
thirty
twenty
wages

TECHNICAL VOCABULARY
ACCOUNT CLERK

ability
abrogate
absence
academic
accept(s)
 (ed) (ance) (ing)
accident(s)
accommodate
accommodating
accompanies
accomplish
accord(ance)
accountant*
accounting*
accounts*
accrual
accrued
accumulate
accurately
achieve(ment)
acknowledge
acquired
acquisition
act(ed)
 (s)
actions
actual*
ad
add*(ing)
 (s)
addends
adequate
adjust(ed)
administer
admission
adopted
advance(s)
advantage(s)
advantageous
advertising
advisable
affect(ing)
affiliated
affirmative
afford

afraid
agencies
agency
agent
agree(ment)
 (s)
aids
aliens
allegation
allocate
allocation
allow(ed)
 (s) (able) (ance)
alternative
amended
amendment(s)
amortized
amounts
ample
analyze
analyzing
annual*(ly)
annuity
answers
apparent
appearing
applicable
application*
applies
apply
appointment
appreciable
appropriate*
approval
approved
arbitrary
arguments
arise
arising
arithmetic
arrangement
arrive
arriving
article(s)
artificial

asking
assembly
assessed
asset(s*)
assign(ed)
 (ment) (s)
assistance
assistant
assisting
assists
associate(d)
assume(s)
assuming
attach(ed)
 (ment)
attempted
attorneys
attributable
audit(ing)
 (or) (s)
authority
authorized
auxiliary
avoid(s)
aware
background
backing
balance*(s)
bank*(s)
bargain(ing)
 (s)
base
beats
becomes
beg
begin
behalf
beneficiary
benefit(ed)
 (ing) (s)
bias
biggest
bilateral
bill(ed)
 (ing) (s)

binary
binding
bit
biweekly
bonds
books
border
borrow(ed)
 (er) (ing)
bought
bound
boundaries
brackets
breach
briefly
bringing
broad
broken
budget(ed)
busiest
businesses*
businessman
buy(er)
 (ing)
bylaws
calculate(d)
calculating
calculation
calculator
calendar
calling
canceled
cancellation
capacities
capacity
capital*
carefully
carload
carry(ing)
cash*
catalog
caused
centralize
cents
certificate

Occupational Literacy Education

challenge
changed
changing
chapter(s)
characteristic
charge(able)
  (d) (s)
charitable
charter
check*(ing)
  (s*)
circular(s)
cited
citizen(s)
civic
civil
claim(ed)
  (s)
clarification
classification
classified
clause
clean(ing)
clear(ed)
  (ing) (s)
clerk
closing
code(d)
  (s)
coding
coin(s)
collect(able)
  (ed) (ion)
column(s)
combination
combined
combining
commerce
commercial
commission
commodities
commonly
communicate
companies
comparable

comparative
compared
comparison
compensation
completed
compliance
complies
comply
compounded
comprehension
comptroller
computation
compute(d)
  (s*)
computer(s)
computing
combination
concentrate
concept(s)
concern(ing)
conclusion
conclusive
condition
conduct(ed)
confidential
confined
conflict
conform
consent
considerable
considerate
consider(ing)
  (s)
consist(ent)
  (s)
consolidate
constitution
construed
consume(d)
  (r)
contact(s)
contained
contains
contemplate
continues

continuity
continuous
contract*(or)
  (s) (ual)
contribute
contribution
control(led)
  (ling) (s)
convention
convert(s)
conveyed
copies
copy
corporate*
corporation*
correct(ion)
  (s)
correspond
council
counsel
count(er)
  (s)
courses
courts
cover(s)
coworkers
create(d)
  (s)
creating
creation
credit*(ed)
  (ing)
creditor(s)
criteria
criticism
crucial
cumulative
currency
custom(ary)
customer(s)
damage(s)
date*(s)
debit(ed)
debt(or)
  (s*)

decimal
decisions
decrease(d)
  (s)
deduct(ed) (ible)
  (ing) (ion) (ions)
deemed
defect(ive)
  (s)
defined
definite
definition
delay(ed)
  (s)
delegation
delinquent
deliver(y)
demand(ed)
denomination
denominator
deny
depend(ent)
  (ing) (s)
deposit(ed)
  (or) (s)
depreciating*
depreciation*
deprive(d)
describes
description
designated
desk
desperate
detail(s)
deter(mination)
  (mines)
determining
devoted
diamond
dictate
differential
difficulty
digits
diligence
dire

directed
directors
disabilities
disability
disagreement
disbursment
disclaim
discount
discovered
discriminate
discuss(ed)
  (ing) (ion)
disposal
disposing
dissolution
dissolve(d)
  (s)
dissolving
distinct
distinguish
distribute
distributing
divest
divide(d)
dividends
dividing
divisor
doctrine
document(s)
dollar(s*)
double
dozen
draft
drawers
drawings
drawn
draws
dues
duplicate
duration
duties
duty
earn(ing)
  (ings)
educational

effecting
efficiently
eight*
eighteen
eighty
elect(ion)
electronic
eleven
eligible
eliminate
emerge
employed
employee(s*)
employers
employs
enable
enact
encumbered
encumbrance
ended
ending
ends
enforce(able)
engage(d)
engaging
enhanced
enjoyed
enriched
enrolled
enter(ed)
  (ing) (s)
enterprise
entertain
entirely
entities
entitle(d)
entity
entries
entry
equal(ly) (s)
equity
errors
essential(ly)
establish(ing)
  (ment)

estate
estimated
estimates
etc.
evenly
event(s)
everybody
evidenced
evident
examination
examine
examples
exceed(ed)
  (s)
exception(s)
excess
exchange
excluding
exclusively
excusable
excuse
executed
execution
executives
executory
exemplified
exempt*(ion*)
  (ions)
exercise
exhibit
exist(ing)
  (s)
expanded
expecting
expects
expenditure
expense*(s*)
explain(ed)
explored
express(ed)
extended
extends
extension
extra
facilitate

facilities
factions
factor
factory
facts
fails
failure
fair
falling
falls
false
familiar
families
fault
favorable
feature(s)
fee(s*)
fifteen
fifty*
figuring
file*(d)
  (s)
filing
filled
finance
financial
finding
finds
finish
firms
fit
fix(ed)
flexibility
flight
flow
follow(s)
forced
forcefully
forever
forget
forgot
formal
formation
formed
formerly

forming	holder	insolvency	juror(s)
formula	holding	inspect(ion)	jury
formulation	hospitals	installment	keeping
forth	hotels	instance(s)	key(punched)
forty	hourly	institution	kinds
forwarded	housecleaning	instruction	label
foundation	housing	instructor	lag
fourteen	hundreds	instrument	laid
fractions	hundredths	insufficient	lately
freely	identical	insurance	latent
freight	illegal	insured	lawful
frequency	illustrate	intangible	laws
frequently	illustrating	intended	lawsuit
Friday	immediately	intent	lawyer
fully	immunities	intercede	laying
functions	impartial	interesting	layovers
fund*(s*)	implied	internal	leagues
furnish(ing)	implies	interpret	learns
gain(ed)	importantly	interstate	leased
gentleman	imposed	intramural	leases
gifts	impossible	intrastate	leaves
giving	impression	introduce(d)	leaving
glue	improper	inventories	ledger
goes	incapacity	inventory*	legal*(ly)
goodbye	incidence	invert	legibly
goodness	included	invest(ed)	legislation
goods	includes	(igate) (ment*)	legislative
gotten	incomes	invisible	legitimate
governing	incorporate	invitation	lender
granted	increases	invite(d)	lending
grants	incurred	invoice(s)	lessee
grocer(y)	incurring	involve(s)	lesson(s)
gross*(es)	indicate(s)	involving	levied
grown	indirectly	irrevocable	liabilities
guarantee(s)	indispensable	issued	liability*
guard	inefficient	issues	liable*
guess	inevitably	issuing	license(d)
guilty	influenced	item*(s)	lifetime
handle	inherent	jobs	limit
happens	inherit	join(t*)	liquid(ation)
hearing	initial	journal	listed
heirs	initiative	judgment	listen(ing)
hence	injuries	July	listing
highest	injury	June	lists
hint	inquiring	juries	literally

literary	mess(ed)	notes	overdraw
litigation	minds	notice(s)	overhead
loan(ed)	minimum(s)	notifies	overtime
(ing)	minute	notify	owe(d)
located	misconduct	null	owned
location	misleading	numbering	owner(s*)
lodging	misnumbered	numerator(s)	(ship)
log	misrepresent	object(ion)	owning
logically	missed	(ive) (ives)	owns
lose	missing	obligated	o'clock
loss(es)	mixed	obligation	package
lowest	modification	observance	packaging
lucky	modified	obtain	packing
lumber	monthly*	occasional	page
machine	motive	occupation	paint
mail	mounting	offer*(ed)	papers
maintain(ed)	multiple	(ee) (or)	paragraph
(ing) (s*)	multiplication	officer(s)	pardon
majority	multiplied	offices	parent
managed	multiplies	official(s)	partial(ly*)
management	multiply(ing)	omission	participant
managerial	mutual	omits	participate
managers	named	operate(d)	parties
manifests	names	(s)	partner*(s*)
manual(ly)	necessarily	operating	(ship*)
manufacture	necessitate	operational	passbook
mark(ed)	necessity	operations	patrons
markdown(s)	negative	operators	payable
marketing	negligence	opposing	payer
markup(s)	neighborhood	opposite	paying
match(es)	net*	option	payment*(s*)
(ing)	nickel	oral	payroll*(s*)
materials	nine*	orders	pays
meant	nineteen	ordinarily	pending
meetings	ninety	ordinary	pension(s)
membership	ninth	ordinates	percent*(age*)
memo	noise	organize(d)	perform(ed)
memorial	non	organization*	(s) (er) (ing)
mental	nonexempt	original	periodic(al)
mentality	nonexistence	ostensible	periods
mentioned	nonprofit	otherwise	permanence
merchandise	noon	ounce	permanent
merchants	normally	outcome	permission
mere	notation(s)	outlined	permits
mergers	noted	outstanding	permitted

perpetual	preserved	purchase*(d*)	reducing
personally	presumed	(r) (s)	refer(red)
pertains	prevailing	purchasing	(s)
petition	prevent	purely	refund
petty	previous(ly)	purports	regard(ing)
philanthropist	prices	purposes*	(less)
phrase	pricing	pursuant	regional
physically	primarily	pursued	register(ed)
pick(ed)	primary	putting	registration
pieces	principal*(s)	qualification	regular(ly)
pink	principles	qualify	regulate(d)
places	prior	quantity	regulating
placing	privileges	quarter(ly*)	regulation
planned	procedure(s)	(s)	reimbursed
please	proceeds	questionable	reimbursement
pledging	processed	quick	reinstate
plenty	processing	quiz(zes)	rejection
plus	produce(d)	radios	related*
pockets	product	raffles	relating
pointed	proficiency	raise	relation(ship)
policies	profit*(able)	random	relative(ly)
portion	(ably) (s)	rapidly	relay
positive	project(ed)	rates	relevant
possibility	(ing) (ion) (s)	ratification	relief
post(ed)	promise(s)	ratified	remain(ing)
(s)	promising	ratify	(s)
potential	promissory	ratio	remedy
pound	promoter(s)	readily	remits
practice	promotes	reasonable*	remittance
preceding	promotional	reasonably	remitted
predominate	proof	receipt(s*)	remitting
preferred	proper(ly)	receivable	remodeled
prejudice	properties	receive(s*)	remunerating
premises	proposed	receiving	render
premium	proprietor*	recognize(d)	rental
prepaid	prospect(us)	recommend(ed)	renting
preparation	protected	reconciles	rents
prepare(d)	protection	recorded	reorganization
(s*)	protest	recorder	replied
preparing	proverbial	recording	reply
prepaying	provides	records	reporting
prerequisite	provision(s)	recover(y)	reports*
presence	prudent	recreation	represent(ative)
presentation	psychological	rectify	reputed
presented	punch	reduce(d)	request*(ed) (s*)

require(ment)
  (s)
requiring
requisition
resale
rescinded
resell
reserve
residence
resident
resolving
resources
respective
responsible
restrict(ed)
  (ion) (s)
resulting
retail(ers)
  (ing) (s)
retained
retains
retention
retired
retiring
returns
revealing
revenue*(s*)
reversals
reverse(d)
reversing
review(ed)
  (s)
revolving
rid
rights
ring
risk(s)
role(s)
rolls
rooms
round
rule(s)
rulings
rush
safe

salaried
salaries
salary
sale*
satisfy
Saturday
save(d) (r)
saving(s)
schedule
scientific
scope
scrapped
secondary
secret
securities
security
sees
seized
seldom
select(ed)
sell*(er)
  (ing*) (s)
semimonthly
send(s)
separate*(ly)
seriously
serves
settlement
seventy
share(d) (s)
shareholder
sharing
sheet*(s)
shelves
shift
shipments
shipped
shipping
shop(s)
showing
shows
sign(ed)
  (ing)
signals
signature

significant
similarly
simplest
sit
situations
sixteen
sixty
skill(fully)
  (s)
skipping
slow
sold*
sole
solution
solve
somebody
somehow
someone
sometime
sorry
sought
sounds
sources
speaking
specialize
specials
specifically
specified
speed
spell(s)
spent
stable
stack
standards
stands
stare
starts
stated
statement(s*)
stating
status
statutes
stipulate(d)
stipulation
stockholder*

stocks
store(s)
strictly
strip
stronger
structure(s)
stub
stuff
style
subchapter
subjects
submits
subscription
subsidiary
substantial
subtotal
subtract(ed)
  (ing) (ion)
success(ful)
sue(d)
suffered
sufficient
suitable
sum(s)
summoned
Sunday
sundries
supermarket
supervision
supervisor
supplier
supply(ing)
supported
suppose(d)
supreme
surfaced
survey
sweater
swimming
switch
tabs
takes
talent(s)
talked
talking

tangible	tonight	uniform	waived
tape	tons	unilateral	waking
tasks	tool	unions	walk
taxability	totally	unique	wants
taxable*	touch	units	warranty
taxation	tourist	unknowingly	watch
taxed	traded	unknown	wealth
taxes*	trade in	unless	wear
taxpayer	trailer	unlike	Wednesday
teach	transact(ion)	unnecessary	weekdays
technically	transfer(red)	unpaid	weekly
technique	(ring) (s)	unrelated	weight
telephone	transit	unused	weird
teller	transported	update	whenever
tells	transposing	useful	whereas
temporary	travel	uses	wherever
tenancy	tribes	utilities	whichever
tenant	truly	utilizes	wholly
tend(ed)	trust(ee)	valid	widely
(s)	(ees) (s)	valuable	willful
tentative	tryout	valuation	willing
term(ed)	Tuesday	valued	win
terminate(d)	tuition	variation	withdrawal
(s)	turning	varies	withdrawn
thank(s)	twelve	variety	withheld
thereafter	twenty*	vary	withholding
thereof	typically	verbal	won
thereon	unaffected	verdicts	wondering
thinks	unanimous	vertical	workers
thirteen	unanticipated	vested	worksheet(s)
thirtieth	unattracting	vinyl	worth(while)
thirty*	unchanged	violating	writer
thorough	unconstitutional	violation	writes
thousand(s)	underlying	virtually	yearly
threw	understand	void	yesterday
throw	undertake	voluntarily	yours
Thursday	undesirable	voting	yourself
tie	unemployment	voucher(s)	zero
timing	unenforceable	wages*	
tomorrow	unfilled	wait	

HIGH FREQUENCY WORDS
AUTO MECHANIC

adjust(ing)
(ment)
alternator
application
armature
assembly
automatic
axle
battery
bearing(s)
bolt
brake
breaker
brush
cable
carrier
certification
circuit
clip
cluster
clutch
coil
column
component
connector
converter
correct
cover
current
customer
describe

diagnosis
diode(s)
disassemble
disconnect
dispensing
dollars
drive(n)
driving
engage
engine
fig.
flows
fluid
fork
fully
gear(s)
hose
housing
identification
ignition
indicator
inspection
install(ation)
(ed)
level
license
loosen
manual
motor
nut
official

oil
operating
output
owner
panel
pedal
pin
pinion
plate(s)
preload
primay
printed
procedure
properly
pull
pump
pushrod
receipt
relay
release
removal
remove(d)
repair
replace
resistance
reverse
ring
screws
seat
secondary
selector

servo
shaft
shift
shock
shop
solenoid
spark
speed
starter
station
steering
switch
teeth
tension
terminal
throttle
thrust
tool
torque
transaxle
transmission
unit
vacuum
valve
vehicle
voltage
washer
wear
wiper
wire
(s)

Occupational Literacy Education

TECHNICAL VOCABULARY
AUTO MECHANIC

absence
absolute
absorbed
absorber(s)
abusing
accelerate
acceleration
accelerator
acceptable
access
accessories
accident(s)
accompanies
accomplish
accumulator
accurately
acid
actions
active
acts
actuators
adapted
adapters
add(ing)
(s)
additives
address
adequate
adjacent
adjust*(ed) (er)
(ing*) (ment*)
admitting
advance
affect
affixed
afford
agent(s)
airflow
align(ed)
(ment) (s)
allow(able)
(ing) (s)
alternating
alternator*
aluminum

ammeter
amounts
amp(s)
amperage(s)
amperes
anchor
angle
announcement
answering
answers
antifreeze
anyway
apart
appears
appliance
applicable
applicant(s)
application*
applied
applies
apply(ing)
appreciable
approaches
approval
approved
approximate
arm
armature
arrange(d)
(ment)
arrived
aside
assemble(d)
assemblies
assembling
assembly*
attach(ed)
(es) (ing)
attacks
attempt(ing)
attendant
attract(ed)
authorized
auto
automatic*

automobile
automotive
avoid
axle*
backed
backing
backs
backward
backyard
ballast
band(s)
bang
bar
basically
bat
batteries
battery*
bay
bearing*(s)
beat
becomes
begin(ners)
(s)
believes
bell
bellhousing
belonging
belt(s)
bench
bending
bendix
besides
bevel
beware
bezel(s)
bias
bicycle
biggest
bind(ing)
bit
bite
blades
blank
blister
block(ing)

blow(ing)
blueprint
bodies
bolt*(ed)
(s)
booklet
boot
booth
bore
bottom
bought
bowl
box
bracket
brake*(s)
braking
branch(es)
brass
breaker*(s)
breathe
brighter
broken
brush*(es)
bubble
buffer
build
buildup
built
bulb
bulk
bureau
burn(ed)
(ing)
burnishing
burred
bushing(s)
busy
butt
button
buy
bypass
cable(s)
calculated
camshaft
cap

carburetor
careful(ly)
carpet
carrier*(s)
carry
cash
casing
catch
caught
caused
causes
causing
caution
centerpunch
centrifugal
certification*
certified
chain
changing
chapter(s)
charged
charger
charging
chart
chassis
cheap
check(ed)
 (ing) (s)
chemical
chipped
choke
circle
circuit*(ry)
 (s)
circulate
circumstance
clamp(ing)
claws
clean(ed)
 (ing)
clearance
clevis
clip(s)
closed
closes

cloth(s)
cluster*
clutch*(es)
coast(ing)
coat
cocked
coefficient
coil*(s)
collapses
collect
colors
column*(s)
combines
combustion
commission
commonly
commutator
compare(d)
comparison
compartment
compensate
complaint(s)
completed
completing
completion
complicate
component*(s)
composition
compress(ed) (es)
 (ing) (ion) (or)
concisely
condensation
condenser
condition(ing)
conducted
conductor(s)
conduit
cone
confuses
confusion
conical
conjunction
connect(ed)
 (ing) (ion)
connector*(s)

considering
consist(s)
console
constant(ly)
constitute
construction
consult(ing)
contact(or)
 (s)
containing
contains
contingency
continually
continuation
continues
continuity
contractor
controlled
controls
convenient
convention
convert(er*)
 (ers)
coolant
cooler(s)
cooling
cooperation
coordinate
copper
copy
core
corporation
correct*(ed)
 (ing) (ly)
correspond
corroded
corrosion
cotton
counterclockwise
countershaft
counting
couples
coupling
courteous
cover*(ed)(s)

cowl
cracks
cranked
cranking
crankshaft
created
critical
cross
cruise
crushed
cup
cupboards
cure
current*
curved
cushion(ing)
customer*(s)
customizing
cycling
cylinder(s)
damage(d)
damping
dart
dash
date
dealer
dealing
deals
decade
deceleration
decreases
decreasing
deduct(ible)
defective
defined
defines
definite(ly)
deflection
deflector
delay
delicate
deliver(ed)
 (s)
demand
demonstrated

dented
dents
depending
depreciating
depress(ed)
  (ing)
depth
describe*
describing
description
designated
destroy(ed)
detach
detail(s)
deteriorate
determines
device(s)
diagnose(d)
diagnosis*
diagnostic
diagram
dial
diameter
diaphragm
differentiate
difficulty
dim
dings
diode*(s*)
dip
dipstick
directing
directs
dirt(y)
disassemble*
disc(s)
discharge
disconnect*
discussed
discussing
disengaged
disk
dispatcher
dispense
dispensing*

display
disposal
disposed
distort(ion)
distribute
distributor
divide(d)
dividing
document
dollar(s*)
domestic(ally)
doors
doped
double
downs
downshift
downward
dozen
drag(ging)
drain(ed)
  (ing)
draw(ing)
  (s)
dressed
drift
drill
drip
drive*(n*)
  (r) (ers)
  (s)
driveshaft
driving*
drop(ped)
  (s)
drum
dry
duct
dust
dustfree
dynamic
earliest
easier
easiest
economy
edge

efficiency
efficient(ly)
eight
elaborate
elbow
electric(al)
electrolyte
electromagnet
electronic
electrons
elemental
eliminate(d)
elite
elsewhere
emerges
emission
empty
enables
ends
energized
energizes
energy
engage*(d)
  (ment) (s)
engine*(s)
engineering
ensure(s)
equal(ly)
equip(ped)
equivalent
essentially
estimate(s)
estimating
etc.
event(s)
  (ually)
everybody
everyday
exact(ly)
examination
examine
exceed(ing)
exception
excess(ive)
  (ively)

exchangers
executive
exempt
exerted
exerting
exhaust
existing
expanding
expensive
expire
explain(ed)
exposed
extended
extending
extends
extension
exterior
external(ly)
extra
extreme
eyebolt
facilitate
facilities
facing(s)
factors
factory
fail(s)
  (ure)
fairly
familiar
fan
farther
fast(ened)
  (er)
fatal
faulty
fee(s)
fenders
fields
fifteen
fifty
fig.*
figuring
file(d)
fill(ed)

film
filter
findings
finger
finished
firewall
firing
firmly
fit(s)
 (ted)
fixed
fixture
flange
flat(s)
flip
float(ing)
floorboard
flow(s*)
fluid*(s)
flush(ed)
 (es) (ing)
flux
fly
flywheel
fog
follow(s)
follow up
foreman
fork*(ed)
formed
forth
forty
forwarded
fraction
frame
freely
freewheel(ing)
freezing
frequency
fresh
friction
frontwheel
fuel(s)
fully*
functioning

functions
furnished
fuse(d)
 (s)
fusible
gain(ed)
gallons
gap
garden
gas(es)
 (sing)
gasket
gasoline
gauge
gear*(ing)
 (s*)
gearset
generalities
generates
giving
glasses
glimpses
governor
grabbing
gravity
grease
grind
gripping
groove(s)
gross
grounded
groundwire
grouped
guess
guesswork
guide
halfway
hamper
handbook
handle(s)
handy
happen(ing)
 (s)
harden
harder

harmful
harness(es)
hatchback
hazard
heading
hearing
heat(er)
heavier
heavy duty
height
helical
herein
hesitant
highways
hoist
holder
holding
holds
hole(s)
hood(s)
hook(ed)
horn
hose*(s)
housing*
hub
hydraulic
hydrogen
hydrometer
ideal
identical
identification
identified
identify(ing)
idler
ignition*(s)
illuminate
illustrate
illustration
imagine
immediately
immerse
impeller
implementing
imported
impossibility

improper
improved
inability
inch(es)
includes
incoming
incorporate
incorrect
increasing
independent
index
indicate(s)
indicating
indication
indicator*
induced
induction
inductive
initiate
injure
in line
inner
inoperative
input
insecticide
insert(ed)
 (ing)
inspect(ed)
 (ion*) (or) (ors)
install*(ation*)
 (ed) (ing)
instuct(ion)
instrument
insulate
insulating
insulation
insulator
insurance
intake
integral
intended
interchange
intercom
intermediate
internal

intervals	leads	lubricant(s)	minor
intricate	leakage	lubricate(d)	minute
introduced	leaking	lubricating	miracle(s)
introduction	leaks	lubrication	mirror(s)
invalid	learn	lug(ging)	missing
inventory	leaves	(s)	mix(ed)
investigation	leaving	lunch	(es)
investment	lengths	machine	mm
invisible	lets	magazine	model(s)
involved	letting	magnet(ic)	mode(s)
isolate	lever*(s)	(s)	modification
isolation	leverage	mainshaft	modified
issued	license*(d)	maintain(ed)	modular
items	(s)	(ing)	modulator
jam	licensing	maintenance	module(s)
jamb	lift	maker	moistened
jammed	lightening	manager	molded
jet	lightly	manifold	molecules
jobs	lights	manual*(ly)	motion
join	lightweight	(s)	motor*(s)
joints	likewise	manufacture	motorcraft
joy(s)	limited	mark(ed)	mount(ed)
jumper	link(age)	(ings) (s)	(ing)
junction	(s)	master	mouth
junk	lint	match	movable
keeps	listed	materially	moves
kerosene	lists	materials	muffler
key(s)	load(ed)	mathematics	multiplication
kick	(s)	matters	names
kill	locate(d)	maximum	nationally
kilometers	locating	meaningful	neatly
kinds	location(s)	measure(d)	necessarily
kit(s)	lock(ed)	(ment)	needing
knob(s)	(s)	measuring	needle(s)
knocked	locknut	mechanic(al)	negative
knocking	lockup	(s)	neighborhood
lab	loose	mechanism(s)	nervous
lacks	loosen*(ed)	melt(ed)	neutral
lamp	(ing)	(s)	nine
latch(es)	loss	mesh(ed)	ninety
lathe	lots	messed	noise(s)
launching	lowered	metal	noisy
lawn	lowering	meter	normally
lbs.	lowers	mile	notch
leading	lowest	mileage	notebook

notice(d)
notification
notifying
noting
nozzle
nut*(s)
nylon
obtaining
occur(red)
  (s)
odometer
offer(s)
officer(s)
official
ohmmeter
oil*(s)
older
opening(s)
operate(d)
  (s)
operating*
operations
operator
opinion
opposing
opposite
option(al)
orders
ordinarily
ordinary
origin
original(ly)
otherwise
outer
outlining
output*
overdrive
overfilling
overhaul(s)
overrevving
override
overrunning
owing
owner*(s)
oxygen

pad
page(s)
pain
paint(ing)
  (s)
pair(s)
pan
panel*
pants
parabolic
paragraphs
parallel
park(ed)
  (ing)
pass(age)
  (ages) (es)
path
patterns
payroll
pedal*
perform
periodical
permanent
permit(s)
  (ting)
petition(er)
phrase(s)
pick(er)
pieces
pin*
pinion*(s)
pink
pinned
pins
pipes
piston(s)
pitch(ed)
pivot
places
placing
planet
planetary
plastic
plate*(s*)
pleasant

pliers
plug(s)
plunger
pockets
pointer
polarity
polish(ed)
portion
positioned
positioning
positions
positive(ly)
possession
possibility
possibly
post
pound(s)
pour
powered
preceding
preferable
preinspect
preliminary
preload*(ed)
preparation
prepare(d)
presented
presized
pressed
presses
pressing
pressure
pretty
prevent
previously
primary*
principles
printed*
prior
prix
probe(s)
procedure*(s)
proceed
produce(d)
  (s)

product
profitable
profit sharing
project
prompt(ly)
proper(ly*)
protect(ive)
  (s)
protrudes
protruding
provides
providing
pry
psi
publish(ed)
pull*(ed)
  (ey) (ing)
pulse
pump*(ed)
  (er) (s)
punch
purchase(r)
purposely
pursuant
push(es)
  (ing)
pushrod*
puts
putting
quadrant
qualified
qualify
qualities
quarter
quick(er)
  (ly)
quiet
quote
race
racing
rag
raise
rapidly
rated
ratings

ratio(s)
rattles
rattling
reach(es)
react(s)
readily
readiness
readjust
reaming
rear
rearward
reasonable
reasonably
reasons
reassemble
reassembly
rebuilt
receipt*
receive(s)
recommend(ation)
    (ing) (s)
reconnect(ed)
recorder
rectifier
recurrence
redone
reduce(s)
reducing
reduction
reface
refer
refinement
reform
refund
regard(less)
registered
registration
regular
regulator(s)
reinforcement
reinspected
reinstall(ation)
    (ed) (ing)
rejected
related

relay*
release*(d)
releasing
remain(der)
    (ing) (s)
reminder
remote(ly)
removal*
remove*(d*)
removing
render
renew
rent
repainting
repair*(ing)
    (s)
repeat(ed)
repel
replace*(d)
    (ment)
replacing
reportable
reposition
representation
reprograming
request(ing)
    (s)
require(ment)
    (s)
requiring
reread
resembles
reservices
reservoir
resin
resist(ance*)
    (or)
resoldering
response
responsible
resting
rests
resulting
retained
retainer

retaining
retard
returns
reverse*
review(ed)
rheostat
ridge
riding
rigor
rim
ring*(s)
rivet
rod
roll
roller(s)
rotate(s)
rotating
rotor(s)
round
row
rpm
rubber
rubble
ruin
rule(s)
rumble
runner
runout
runs
sacrificing
safety
sale
salesman(ship)
salesroom
sample
satisfied
save
scale
schematic
scientific
score
screw(s*)
screwdriver
seal
seat*(ed)(s)

seatbelt
secondary*
sections
secure(d)
    (ly)
securing
seeing
sees
seizing
select(ing)
    (ive) (or*)
self
sell
send(ing)
sentence(s)
separate(ly)
sequence
seriously
serve(s)
serviced
servicing
servo*(s)
setscrew
setting
settle
severe
shaft*(s)
sheet
shelves
shield(s)
shift*(ed)
    (er) (ing) (s)
shock*
shooting
shop*(s)
shorted
shorten
shoulder
showing
shows
shunt
shut
sideplay
sides
sign(ed)

simplicity	specification	strut(s)	tested
simplify	specifics	stuck	tester
simultaneously	speed*(s)	stud	testing
sits	speedometer	studies	tests
sixty	spillage	stuff	thank(s)
sizes	spilled	stupid	thereof
skills	spinning	sufficient	thick(ness)
slack	spiral	suitable	(es)
slammed	splined	sulfuric	thin(ner)
sleeve	splines	sum	thirty
slid	split	superceded	thorough(ly)
slide	spoke	superintend*	thousand
slightest	springs	supplied	thread(ed)
slightly	sprocket(s)	supply	(s)
slip(page)	spun	suppression	throttle*
(pery)	squeezed	surfaces	throw
slipring	squirting	surges	thrust*
slot(s)	stages	surprised	thicket
(ted)	stainless	suspect	tighten(s)
slower	stamped	suspension	tightly
sludge	stands	swelled	till
smaller	starter*	switch*(ing)	tilt(ed)
smallest	starting	symbols	timely
smooth(ly)	starts	symptom(s)	timing
snap	station*(s)	synchronize	tip(s)
snow	stationary	tab(bed)	tire
snugly	stator	(s)	title
soaked	steady	tackle	toe
socket(s)	steam	tail	tool*(s)
sold	steel	tailored	toploader
solder(ing)	steering*	takes	torn
solenoid*(s)	stem	talked	torque*
solid	sticker	talking	touch(ed)
solution	stirring	tangs	(ing)
solvent	stops	tank	tougher
somehow	storage	tap	toward
someone	storeroom	tape	tower
somewhere	straighten(ed)	teardown	towing
sounding	strand	technician	trace(s)
source(s)	strap	technology	track
spaced	strictly	teeth*	trailer
spacer	strip	tend(ency)	train(s)
sparingly	stroke(s)	tension*	transaxle*
spark*	strongly	term(inal*)	transfer(red)
specifically	struck	(inals)	transforms

transistor	underneath	version	whenever
transmission	unhook	vertical	whereas
transmits	uniform	vibration	wherever
travel	unique	viewed	whoever
treat(ed)	unit*(s)	virtue	wiggles
trend	unitized	viscosity	winding(s)
trick	unkown	vise	windshield
triggering	unlawful	volt(age*)	wipe(d)
trim	unless	wagons	(r*)
troubles	unlike	wait	wire*(s*)
truck	unlimited	wander	wiring
trunks	unsolder	wants	wise
tuneup	updated	ward(s)	withdraw
turbine	upper	warn(er)	(n)
turbo	upright	(ing)	withstand
turning	unshift	warped	wonder(ing)
turns	uses	warranty	workbench
twelve	utmost	wash(ed)	workshop
twenty	vacuum*	(er*) (ers)	worn(out)
twisted	valid	watch	worry
twisting	validity	waved	worth
twitch	valve*(s)	wax	wrap
typical	vanes	weak(ened)	wrench
unavailable	variable	wear*(ing)	yellow
unbolted	vary(ing)	(s)	yoke
uncovering	vaseline	weighed	yours
undergoing	vehicle*(s)	wet	zero
undergone	venerable	wheel(s)	zinc

HIGH FREQUENCY WORDS
DRAFTSMAN

ac
all right
base
bean
brick
buildings
component
concrete
connection
construction
diameter
dimension(s)
draw(ing)
  (ings) (n)
eight
elevation

equal
exterior
feature(s)
fifty
fig.
foot
foundation
ft.
grid
harness
heads
heat
horizontal
inch(es)
inspection
intersection

joint(s)
layout
location
manufacture
materials
metal
object
openings
panel(s)
parallel
pipe
plate
radiograph
requirement
sheet
specification

specified
steel
tension
thickness
tolerance
twelve
twenty
vertical
vessel
  (s)
walls
weld(ed)
  (s)
wire(s)
wiring
wood

Occupational Literacy Education

TECHNICAL VOCABULARY
DRAFTSMAN

ability
abrasion
abreast
absence
absorption
abutting
ac*
accelerate
acceleration
acceptability
acceptable
acceptance
accepted
access
accommodate
accomplish
accordance
accumulating
accuracy*
accurate
achieved
achieving
acoustical
acquaintance
acquainted
acquire
acted
acting
acts
actual
ad
adaptable
add(ing)
(s)
address(er)
(es)
adequate(ly)
adhesive
adjacent
adjustment
admission
adopt(ed)
advantage(s)
advent
aesthetic

affect
affixed
aircraft
airspeed
album(s)
aligned
alignment
all
allocated
allocation
allow(able)
(ance) (ances)
alloy
alteration
alternative
altitude
aluminum
amended
amendment
amounts
anchor(s)
angle(d)
(s)
angular(ity)
annex
annular
answers
apart
apiece
apparatus
appearance
appendices
appendix
applicable
application
applies
apply(ing)
appreciate
appropriate
approved
approximate
arbitrarily
arbitrary
arc
arched

arches
architect(s)
(ure)
arm
arranged
arrangement
arrived
arriving
arrow
artistry
artwork
aside
assembly
assignment
assistants
assume(d)
assuming
assumption
assurance
atmospheric
attach(ed)
(ment)
attain
attempted
attics
auction
automated
automatic
automation
avoid
await
awake
aware
awful
axes
axis
background
backing
backup
bacterial
balloon
bank
bar
barely
barrier

base*(s)
baseball
baseboards
basically
basketball
batch
battery
bay
beam*(s)
beans
bear(able)
beat(s)
becomes
beforehand
beg
begin
bell
bellmouth
bench
bend(ing)
beneath
beneficial
besides
bet
bevel(ed)
beware
bilateral
binders
binding
bisect(ing)
(ors)
bit
blade
blasted
block(ing)
(s)
blow(s)
boards
boiler(s)
bolted
bolts
bond
books
boom
bosses

bottom
boundary
bow
bowls
boxes
braced
braces
bracing
branch(es)
breadth
break(ing)
    (s)
breeching
brick*(ed)
    (s)
bridge
brief(ly)
broad
broke
build(er)
    (ers) (ings*)
built
bulkheads
bundle
burn
busy
butt
button
buy
bye
cabinet
cable
cages
calculate(d)
    (s)
calculating
calculation
calculus
calling
canceled
cancels
cantilever
capable
capacities
capacity

cape
capital
carbon
career
careful(ly)
carpenters
carport
carrier
carry(ing)
Cartesian
cash
casings
cast(s)
cataloged
catalogs
catch
categories
category
caulking
caused
causes
causing
cavity
cedar
ceiling(s)
celebrating
centers
centimeter
centroid(s)
centuries
certificate
cesspool
chair
chalk
challenge
challenging
chambers
chances
changed
channel
chap
chapter(s)
characteristics
charts
chassis

check(ing)
cheek
chimney
choose
chose
chutes
circle(s)
circuit(ry)
circular
circumference
civil
clad
clamped
clamps
classification
classified
clay
clean(ed)
    (ing)
clearance(s)
client
clip
closely
closest
closing
closure
cm
coal
coast
coat
coaxiality
code(s)
coffee
coincided
coke
collective
colonial
colors
columns
combination
combustible
combustion
commercial
commonly
communicate

comparative
comparison
compass
compensation
competent
completed
completing
completion
complex
complicate
compliment
comply(ing)
component*(s)
composed
composition
compressed
compression
computation
computed
conclave
concealed
concentrate
concentric
concept
concern(ing)
concrete*
concurrent
condensate
condensation
condition
conductor(s)
cone(s)
confidence
confines
conflict
conform
confusion
conical
conjunction
connect(ed)
    (ing) (ion*) (ors)
conservation
considerate
consist(ent)
    (s)

constant(ly)
constituent
constructed
construction
consultation
consults
contact(ed)
  (s)
contain(ed)
  (s)
contemporary
continuous
contour(ed)
  (s)
contraction
contractor
contrasting
contribute
controlled
controlling
controls
convenient
convention
conversation
conversion
convert
cool(ing)
coordinate
coordination
cope
copies
copper
copy
cord
cores
corners
cornice
correct(ly)
correspond
corridor
corrosion
corrosive
cosign
counseling
counselors

couplings
courses
cousin
cover(age)
  (ing) (ings) (s)
cracking
cracklike
cracks
crane(s)
create(d)
  (s)
creativity
crimp
criteria
critical
cross(ing)
crossline
cross section
crosswalks
crowbars
crown
crunch
cube
cubic
curbs
currently
curtain
curve(d)
custom(ary)
cuts
cutting
cycle
cylinder(s)
cylindrical
damage(d)
dampened
dash
date(s)
datum
daytime
dc
dealer
dealing
deals
debated

debris
deceleration
decent
decimal(ly)
deck
decoration
defects
define(s)
defied
defining
definitely
definition
deflection
deform
degrees
delineated
deliver(y)
denominator
denotes
density
depend(ing)
deposit
depression
depth
derived
describe
description
descriptive
designate(d)
designation
designer(s)
designing
designs
desirable
desired
desk
destruction
detail(ed)
  (s)
detergents
determining
develop(ing)
device(s)
devoted
dew

diagonal(ly)
diagram(s)
diameter*(s)
die
differ(s)
difficulties
difficulty
dim
dimension*(ed)
  (ing) (s*)
dinner
directed
directions
director
discharge
discuss(ed)
disposal
disposed
distances
distinguish
disturbing
diver
divide(d)
dividing
divisions
document
dollars
domestic
doorknob
dot(ted)
double
doubts
downstairs
downtown
downward
draft(ing)
draftsman
drain(age)
  (s)
draw*(ing*)
  (ings*) (n*)
dress
drilled
drinks
drippings

driven
driver
drives
driveways
driving
drop(ped)
 (s)
drove
dry
duct(s)
ductwork
dug
dumbwaiter
durable
dusting
dwelling
dynamic(s)
easier
eating
eaves
eccentric
economical
economy
edge
editions
effectively
efficiency
effluent
eight*
eighteen
eighty
elaborate
elbow(s)
electrical
electronic
elevation*(s)
eleven
eliminate(s)
ellipse
elliptical
elongation
embedded
emphasis
emphasized
employed

employees
emptied
empty
enclose(d)
enclosure(s)
encountered
ending
ends
energy
engineer(ing)
enjoyed
ensure
entail(s)
entering
enters
enthusiasm
entirely
entrance
environment
equal*(ly)
 (s)
equation(s)
equilibrium
equipped
equivalent
erase
erect(ing)
 (ion)
erosion
escalator(s)
essential
establish(ing)
estimate(s)
etc.
evenly
event(ually)
 (s)
evolved
exact(ing)
 (ly) (ness)
exam(ination)
 (ined)
examples
excavation
exceed(ing) (s)

exception(s)
exchange
excluded
excuse
exempted
exercise(s)
exert(s)
exhaustive
exist
exit(s)
expanded
expanse
expansion
expensive
explain(ed)
 (s)
explanatory
exposed
expressed
expressing
extend
 (ing)
extension
exterior*
external
extinguish
extra
extreme
eyelets
fabricated
fabrication
facing
factor
failure
fairly
falling
falls
false
familiar
fan(ned)
fancy
fantastic
farmer
fasten(ed)
 (ing)

favor(ites)
feasible
feature*(s*)
February
feeder
fewer
fiber
fields
fifteen(th)
fifth(s)
fifty*
fig.*
fights
figured
figuring
file(d)
 (s)
filled
fillet
finding
fingers
finish(ed)
 (ing)
firebrick
fireplace
firmly
fit(s)
fitting(s)
fixed
fixtures
flame
flammability
flange(d)
 (s)
flashing
flat
flight
flooring
floors
flow
flue
flush
flux
fly
foam

folder
folding
follow(s)
foot*(ing)
foregoing
foreshorten
forged
forget
forging
format
formed
formerly
forming
formula(s)
forth
forty
foundation*
fourteen
fourth(s)
foyer
fractions
frame(s)
framing
fraternal
freebody
freed
freehand
freely
frequently
friction
Friday
fronting
ft.*
fully
fun
fundamental
funny
furnished
furniture
fur(red)
(ring)
fusion
gable(s)
gaging
gallon(s)

galvanized
games
gap
gas(eous)
(es) (sed)
gauge(s)
gear
generated
gently
geometric(al)
gets
girders
giving
glass
goal
goes
gold
gotten
govern(ing)
(s)
grade
graduates
graphical
gravel
gravity
grid*
grooves
grout
guarded
guess
guide(s)
guys
gypsum
gyration
hallway
hammer
handbook
handed
handhole(s)
handicap
handle
handrails
hang
happen(s)
happy

hardware
harness*
haul
headers
heads*
hearth
heat*(ed)
(er) (ers) (ing)
heaviest
heel
height
hereof
hereunder
hidden
highly
holdage
holders
holding
hole(s)
homes
homework
hook
hopefully
horizon
horizontal*
houses
housing
hub(s)
hungry
hurt
hydraulic
hypotenuse
identical
identification
identified
identify(ing)
illustrate
illustration
impact
impending
implies
implying
impossible
impractical
impression

improve
inaccurate
inch*(es*)
inclined
included
inclusive
incomplete
inconsistent
incorrectly
increases
increasing
increment
incurred
indentation
independent
indicate(s)
indicating
indication
indicator
indirectly
inertia
inherent
initial
inner
inspection*
inspector
installation
installed
instances
institute
institution
instruction
instructor
instrument
insulating
insulation
insurance
integrally
intended
intent(ional)
interboard
interconnect
interesting
interests
interfere(nce)

interfering	lands	load bearing	mechanical
interior(s)	lap(ped)	locate(d)	mechanism
intermediate	(s)	locating	medium
internal	largely	location*(s)	meets
interpretation	lath	lock(ing)	mental(ly)
interpreted	laundry	logical	merits
interpreting	layer	longitudinal	mesh
interrelated	laying	looks	message
intersect(ed)	layout*(s)	loosened	metal*
(ion*)	lb.	looseness	meter(ing)
interval(s)	leading	lose	(s)
introduced	leads	losing	metric
introduces	leaked	losses	mile
inventory	leaking	lowest	millimeter
irregular	lease	lucky	mineral
isolated	leaves	lumber	miniaturize
isolation	leaving	lunch	minimize
items	ledger	lyrics	minimum
jambs	ledges	machine(d)	minus
jobs	leg(s)	(ry) (s)	minute
join(ed)	lengths	magnetic	miter(s)
(ing)	lesser	magnifies	mm
joint*(ed)	leveled	magnitude	modification
(s*)	levels	magnolia	modular
joist(s)	liability	mail	module
judging	librarian	mainly	moisture
jumper	libraries	maintain(ed)	moldings
jumps	library	(s)	molds
justification	lieu	manhole	moments
keeping	lift(ing)	manhours	Monday
keeps	lights	manpower	monetary
key	liked	manufacture*	moon
kg	limit(ing) (s)	mark(ing)	moreover
kilograms	linear	masonry	mornings
kit	lined	master	mortar
kitchen	liner(s)	matching	motion
knocking	lining(s)	materials	motivated
knows	lip	math	mountains
labeled	liquid	mating	mounted
laboratories	listed	matrix	mounts
laborers	listen(ing)	maximum	movable
lacking	lists	meanings	mph
laid	lives	measure(d)	mud
landed	load(ed)	(ment) (s)	multiple
landing	(ing) (s)	measuring	multiplied

multiply(ing)
mutual
nail(ed)
    (ing) (s)
naturally
nearby
nearest
neat(ly)
necessarily
necessitate
necessity
neck(s)
negative
neglecting
negligible
net
newtons
nice
nine
nineteen
ninety
nobody
noise
nominal
noncombustible
noncomplex
noncorrosive
normally
notch(ed)
noted
notes
notice(able)
nozzle(s)
numbered
numerators
numerical
object*(s)
objectionable
obstruction
obtain
obvious
occasion
occupancies
occupancy
occupant(s)

occupied
occur
octagon
offering
offices
official
offset(s)
    (ting)
ogee
oil
ok
omitted
onto
opening(s*)
opens
operable
operate
operations
operator
opposed
opposes
opposing
opposite
ordered
organized
original
otherwise
ought
outer
outlet(s)
outline(d)
output
overall
overhang(s)
overhead
overlap(ping)
overtaken
overwork
owner
pack(age)
page(s)
pain
painted
panel*(ing)
    (ized) (s*)

papers
parachute
paragraph(s)
parallel*
pardon
partially
particle
parties
partition(s)
partly
pass(es)
    (ing)
patched
path(s)
patio
patterns
penalties
penetrant
penetration
penthouses
percent(age)
perforated
performed
performing
perimeter
permanent
permissible
permit(s)
    (ted)
perpendicular
personnel
perspective
pertain(ing)
physically
pi
pick(ed)
    (ing) (s)
pictorial
pieces
pier(s)
pigtail
pinned
pins
pipe*(s)
piping

pit
places
placing
plain
planer(s)
planes
planned
plaster
plastic(s)
plate*(d)
    (s)
platforms
plated
playing
plot(ted)
    (ting)
plug(ged)
plumb(ed)
    (ing)
plus
plywood
printing
policies
popular
porcelain
porch
port(able)
portion(s)
posed
positional
positioned
positions
positive
possibility
possibly
postal
potential
pounds
poured
practical
practice(s)
precedence
precipitate
precisely
precision

predetermine	prove(d)	reduce(d)	respects
predrilled	(n)	reduction	restricted
preferably	provides	redwood	restrooms
preferred	providing	refastened	rests
preheating	provision(s)	refer(red)	resulting
preliminary	psi	(ring)	retaining
preparation	pull(ed)	reference(d)	retardant
prepared	pulse	regardless	reveal(ing)
preparing	punched	registered	reverse
preplan	purchase	registrars	review
prescribed	purposes	regular	rewards
present day	pursued	reinforced	rig
presents	pushed	reinforcement	right
pressing	putting	reinforcing	ring(s)
pressures	quadrant(s)	relate(d)	ripped
prevailing	quantities	relation(ship)	rise
prevent(s)	quantity	relative(s)	roads
previous	quarter(s)	release(d)	rocks
prices	quick(er)	(s)	rod
primarily	(ly)	reliable	rolled
principles	radiant	remain(ing)	roof(s)
printed	radiograph*	remodeling	rooms
printing	radius	removable	root
prints	rails	remove(d)	rope
prior	raised	removing	rough
procedures	ramp	repair(ed)	round(ed)
proceed	ramset	(s)	rule(s)
processes	random	replaced	runs
processing	rapid	represent(ed)	safe(ty)
produce(d) (s)	rates	(s)	salvaged
product	rating	requesting	salvation
proficient	raw	require(ment*)	sample
profile(s)	reactions	(s)	satellite
progresses	readily	requiring	satisfactory
prohibit	realistic	requisition	satisfied
project(ed)	realize	resembling	Saturday
(ing) (ion)	reasonable	reserved	scale
promised	reasons	reserves	scaling
proof	rebound	reservoir(s)	schedule(d)
proper(ly)	recessed	residence(s)	schematics
proportion	recommended	residential	scissors
propose	recorded	resistance	scratch
prospective	rectangle(s)	resistive	screen
protect(ed)	rectangular	resolve	screws
(ion)	redesign	respective	scribed

script	shift(s)	slightly	staggered
sealed	shingles	slipped	stainless
sealer	ship(ment)	slope(s)	stairways
seam	shoot	slots	stamped
searching	shop	slow	standards
seated	shorted	slug	standing
seating	shortest	smaller	standpoint
secondary	should	smoke(y)	starter(s)
seconds	showcases	smooth(ly)	starting
sectional(s)	showing	snap(ped)	starts
sections	shows	socket	stated
secured	shrink	soil	static(s)
securely	sides	sold	stating
securing	sidewalk(s)	solder	stationery
seep(age)	siding	solid	statistics
seldom	signal(s)	solution	stays
selected	significant	solve(d)	steam
selecting	signify	solving	steel*
selection	sill(s)	sooner	steep
self	similarly	source(s)	stenograph
selling	simplest	spaced	stepping
semicircle	simplification	spaces	stick(ing)
semidiameter	simultaneous	spacing	stiffen
send	singing	span	stocked
separate(d)	singular	spandrels	stone
separation	sit(ting)	spec	stopper
septic	site	specialize	stops
serves	situations	specifically	storage
serving	sixteen(th)	specification*	store(s)
setting	sixth	specified*	storm
settling	sized	specify(ing)	strap(s)
seventy	sizes	specimen(s)	streets
sewage	sizing	spell	strengths
sewer	sketch(ed)	spend	stresses
shade	(es) (ing)	spherical	stretch
shadow(s)	skids	spiral	strike
shaft(s)	skilled	short	striking
shakes	sky	spot(ting)	strings
shape(d)	skylights	spread	strip(ped)
(s)	slab(s)	sprinklers	(s)
sheet*(ing)	slanted	squared	struck
(s)	sledge	squares	structural
shell(ed)	sleeper	squaring	structure(s)
(s)	sleeping	stability	studies
shield	slide(rs)	stable	stuff

style
sub
subcontract
subdivision
subgrade
subjected
subjects
subparagraph
subsection
subsequent
substances
substantial
substitute
substituting
successful
sufficient
suggest(ion)
suitable
sum
supervisor
supper
supplement
suppliers
supply
supported
suppose(d)
surfaces
surprised
surrounded
surrounding
surveying
suspended
switch
symbol(s)
symmetrical
symmetry
tables
tabs
tack welding
tag
tail
takeoff
takes
talked
talking

tally
tamped
tangent
tank(s)
tape(d)
taper(ed)
  (ing) (s)
target
task
team
techniques
tee(s)
telephone
temporarily
temporary
tenant
tend(s)
tensile
tension*
tentative
tenth
term
terminal(s)
terminate(s)
termination
testing
tests
text(s)
textural
texture(s)
theorem
theoretical
thereby
therein
thereof
thereto
thick(er)
  (ness*) (nesses)
thinner
thirteen
thirty
thorough(ly)
thousand
thread(ed)
throat

throw(s)
thorough
thumbnail
Thursday
tie(d)
  (s)
tighten
tightly
tightness
tile
till
timber
tiny
tip(ping)
title
toe
toilet
tolerance*(s)
tomorrow
tons
tool(ed)
totaled
touchup
trace(d)
tracing
tracks
trades
traditional
traffic
trailer(s)
trained
transfer
transition
transportation
transverse
trapezoid
traveling
treated
treatments
trench(es)
trend
triangle(s)
triangulate
trim(mers)
truck(s)

truss(es)
tube(s)
tubing
tune
twelve*
twenty*
twice
twisted
twisting
typical
ultrasonic
unacceptable
unacquainted
unbalanced
unbearable
uncle
uncontrolled
undercarriage
undermining
underneath
undimensioned
unenclosed
uneven
unfired
unforseeable
unified
uniform(ly)
unilateral
unit(s)
unknown(s)
unless
unloading
unnecessary
unproductive
unprotected
unstayed
unsupported
unusual(ly)
unwieldly
upper
upset
upward
usable
useful
usual

vacation	vitreous	weight(s)	withstand
valley	vitrified	weld*(ed*)	won
vanish(es)	void	(er) (ing)	wonder
(ing)	volts	(s*)	wood*
vaporizer	volumes	wheeler	wool
variables	wainscoting	wheeling	worker
variation(s)	wait	whereas	(s)
variety	wales	wherever	workmanship
vary(ing)	walk	whoever	worksheet
vault(s)	wallboard	widely	worry
vector(s)	walls*	wider	worse
velocity	wants	width(s)	wrap(per)
veneer(s)	warrant	win	wrecked
vents	waster	wind	wrench
verge	wasted	windlift	yards
verify	wastes	windows	yell
vertical*(ly)	wedge	windstorm	yellow
vessel*(s*)	weekend	winter	yesterday
violation	weighed	wire*(s*)	zero
virtual	weighs	wiring*	zone

HIGH FREQUENCY WORDS
ELECTRICIAN

accordance
approved
article
axis
bar
behavior
box(es)
cable
charges
circuit(s)
code
coil
conductor(s)
conduit

connect(ed)
contract(or)
core
crisis
electric(al)
equation(s)
etc.
feeder
fixture
flexible
graph
grounded
grounding
installation

iron
jumper
liquid
load
locations
magnetic
materials
metal
meter
motor
ohms
outlet
permitted
rating

relay
resistance
resistor
sizes
solution
specification
specified
terminal(s)
thousand
unknown
volt(age)
  (ages) (s)
wire
wiring

Occupational Literacy Education

abilities
ability
abnormal
absence
acceptable
acceptance
accepting
access(ible)
accident(s)
accompanying
accomplish
accordance*
accumulating
accuracy
accurate(ly)
achieve(d)
  (ment)
activated
actual
actuate
additions
adequacy
adequate
adhesive
adjacent
adjusted
adjusting
adjustment
admired
adult(s)
advanced
advice
affect(ed)
  (s)
affixed
afterward
agency
aggregate
air conditioning
alarm(s)
algebraic
allow(ing)
  (s)
alloys
alnico

alteration
altered
alternate
alternating
altitude
aluminum
ambient
amendatory
amp
ampacity
ampere(s)
amplifier(s)
analyze
angle(s)
annunciator
anticipate
antimony
apathetic
apparatus
appliance(s)
applicable
application
applies
apply
apprentice
approached
appropriate
approved*
approximate
architect(s)
  (ure)
arise
arithmetic
arm
armature
arranged
arrangement
arrow
article*(s)
assembled
assemblies
assembly
assistance
associate(d)
atoms

attached
attachment
attaining
attempt
attendant
attitudes
attributed
authority
automated
automatic(ally)
automobile
avenue
avoid
axes
axial
axis
balance
ballast(s)
bands
bar*(s)
bare
barrier
base(ments)
battery
bear
beating
becomes
begins
behavior
beings
bell
bench
bet
bias
bid(der)
  (ders) (ding)
bigger
biggest
biological
bipolar
bismuth
bit
blade
blanked
block(s)

blowing
bodies
bond(ed)
  (ing)
books
boom
boring
bottle
bottom
bounced
bows
box*(es*)
braced
brain(s)
brainstorm
brake
branch(es)
break(er)
  (ing) (s)
bringing
brings
brother
built
burn(ed)
bus
bushing(s)
butterfly
buy(er)
  (ing)
buzz
cab
cabinet(s)
cable*(s)
calculate(d)
calculation
calculator
calibrated
calibration
calls
canceling
canopies
capacities
capacitive
capacitor
careful(ly)

carriers
carries
carry(ing)
cast
catalog
catatonic
category
caused
causes
causing
ceiling(s)
Celcius
cemented
cementing
centers
chair
chalk
chances
changed
changing
chapter(s)
characteristic
charged
charges*
charging
chart
chases
chassis
chatter
check(ed)
(ing) (s)
chewed
choose
choosing
chosen
chromium
circuit*(s*)
circulate(s)
cited
claim
clamping
classed
classes
classification
classified

clean(ed)
(ing)
cleared
climates
climb
closely
closer
closures
clothed
cobalt
code*(s)
coefficient
coil*(ed)
(s)
collector
collision
columns
comb
combination
combined
combustible
comfort(able)
commercial
companies
comparable
compare(d)
complaining
completed
completion
complex
compliance
comply
component(s)
composition
compressed
compression
compressor
computation
computed
computer
concealed
concentrate
concept(s)
concise
concrete

condition(ing)
conduct(ion)
(or*) (ors*)
conductive
conduit*(s)
confidence
conflict
conform
confused
connect*(ed*)
(ion) (s)
considerable
considerate
considering
considers
consist(ent)
(ing) (s)
constant(s)
constitute
construct(ing)
consumes
contact(s)
contain(ed) (er)
(ers) (ing) (s)
contentment
continuous
contract*(or*)
(s)
contribute
controlled
controller
controls
convenient
conveyors
cooling
cools
cooperate
coordinate
coordination
cope
copper
copy
cord(s)
core*
correct(ed) (ion)

correlation
correspond
corrosion
costly
counting
coupling
courses
cover(s)
crescent
crises
crisis*
crisscross
critical
cross
crowd(ed)
crystal
curie
currently
currents
curve
customer
cuts
cutting
cycle
damage(d)
(s)
dangerous
dangers
date(s)
dc
dealing
decimal
de-energize
defined
defining
definition
deflection
degrees
delay
delivered
delivery
demagnetize
demand
demolition
demonstrate

denominator	distinguish	effectiveness	evaluates
density	distorts	eight	evaluation
depend(ency)	distributing	elect	event(ually)
(ent) (ing) (s)	diversity	electric*(al*)	evident
deposits	dives	(ian) (ity)	exact(ly)
depth	divided	electrode(s)	exam(ine)
derived	divider(s)	electromotive	(ples)
description	documents	electron(ic)	excavators
designating	dodge	(s)	exceed(ing)
designation	dollar(s)	element	exception
desired	dominated	elevator	excess(ive)
detail	doors	eliminate(d)	excluding
detect(or)	doses	elsewhere	exclusive
deteriorate	dotted	embarrassment	excuse
determinant	double	embedded	execution
determining	drag	emergency	executive
develop(ing)	draglines	emf	exhaust(ed)
(s)	drain	emotional(ly)	exist(ing)
device(s)	draw(ing)	emphasis	(s)
diagram(matic)	(ings) (n)	employed	expands
(s)	dredges	empty	expense
die	dressed	enclosed	experiencing
dielectric	dribble	enclosure(s)	experiment
differently	dried	encountered	explain(ed)
differing	drift	energize(d)	explosions
dimensional	drills	energy	exposed
dip	drips	engages	expressing
directed	drives	engineering	expression
dirt	driving	engineers	expressly
disagreement	drop(ped)	engraved	extended
disassociate	(s)	enhances	extensive
discharge	drove	enter	external
disconnect	drum(s)	entrance	extra
discourage	dry	envelope	extremes
discovered	dual	environment	facilities
discussed	duct(s)	equal(s)	factor
discusses	dug	equation*(s*)	failure
discussing	dull	equipment	false
disease	dumped	equivalent	familiar
disintegrate	dust	erratic	families
dislike(s)	dynamic	errors	fan
disorder	easier	escape	fascinating
display	economy	essential(ly)	fast
disputable	edition	estimate	fastened
distinct	effectively	etc.*	fault

favor(able)
fears
feature
fed
feedback
feeder*(s)
ferromagnet
fiberglass
fields
fifteen
fifth
fig.
figured
filing
fill
filtered
financial
finding
finds
finish(ed)
 (es)
fireplace
fires
fit(ting)
 (tings)
fixture*(s)
flammable
flattened
flexible*
floatless
floors
flow(s)
fluids
flush
flux
focus
follow
fool
foot(ing)
forced
foregoing
formula
forth
forty
fourth

fraction(al)
 (s)
frame
freezing
frequency
frequently
Friday
frozen
frustrating
frustration
fullscale
fully
fume
functional
functioning
functions
fundamental
furnishes
furnishing
furthermore
fuse(s)
gage
gallons
galvanized
games
gases
gasoline
gauge
gear
generate(d)
generating
generation
generator(s)
gets
giving
glad
glandular
glass
goes
gold
govern(ing)
grade
gradual
graph*(s)
grass

grease
grids
grinned
grounded*
grounding*
grout
grow(s)
guarantee
guard(ed)
guess
guide(lines)
guns
gutter(s)
habits
hallway
handbook
handicap
handle
handout
handy
hanger
hanging
happening
happens
happiness
harm
hazardous
heat(er)
heat-reacting
height
hence
herein
hertz
high(er)
 (est)
highpower
hill
hoists
holder
holds
hole(s)
hoods
hook
horizontal
horsepower

hostile
hp
humidity
hundredth
hypotenuse
identify(ing)
identity
illustrate
imbalance
immeasurable
immediately
impedance
impression
improper
inaccessible
inadequate
incessantly
inch(es)
incidental
included
includes
inconvenient
increases
increasing
incurred
independent
indicate
indication
indoor
induction
inductive
inductor
inexpensive
influenced
influences
informal
informed
initial
inoperative
input
inquiry
insert
inspection
inspector
installation*

installed	junction	limiting	maternal
instance(s)	keen	linear	mathematic
instant	keeping	lingering	mature(s)
instinct(ive)	kicked	lining	maturing
instruction	kidding	link	maturity
instrument	kill	liquefied	maximum
insulated	kilo(gram)	liquid*(s)	measure(d)
insulating	kinds	listed	(ment) (s)
insulation	knock(out)	listing	measuring
insulator	(outs)(s)	literal	mechanical
integers	kw	lives	mechanism
integral	lab	load*(s)	median
intellectual	label(ed)	located	meets
intense	(ing)	location(s*)	melting
intent	laboratories	lock(ed)	memory
interact(ion)	laboratory	logical	mental(ly)
interchange	lag(s)	longest	mention
interference	laminated	looped	mercury
interior	lamp(s)	loosely	merit
interlocks	lampholder	loosen	message
internal	largest	loses	messed
interrupting	lash	losing	metal*
intersection	lately	loss	meter*(s)
intervals	latest	low	mezzanine
interwoven	lattice	lug(s)	microsecond
intolerable	laws	machine(d)	mil
introduce(d)	layout(s)	magazines	milli
introducing	lays	magnet(ic*)	mine
introduction	lcd	(ism)	minimum
inverted	lead in	(ized)	minority
investigate	leading	(izing)	minute
invisible	leads	magnitude	misaligned
invited	leakage	mainly	missed
involve(ment)	leaking	maintain(ed)	missing
(s)	leaves	(ing)	mistake
involving	legs	(s)	mistuned
iron*	lessen	majority	misunderstand
irritability	lesser	manage	misused
isolated	liability	mandrel	mixed
item(s)	lifetime	manganese	mobile
jacket(ed)	lighting	manual	moderate
jerk(ed)	lights	manufacture	moisture
joint(s)	liked	mark(ed)	molecular
judgment	likes	marriage	molecules
jumper*	limitation	materials*	moreover

motion	offensive	parallel(ed)	polarities
motivated	officials	paralysis	polarity
motivation	offset	paresis	pole
motives	ohm(meter) (s*)	park	polynomial
motor*(s)	oil	partially	popular
mounted	older	pass(ing)	porches
movable	opening(s)	pasted	portable
ms	operate(d)	patching	portal
multimotor	operating	path	portion(s)
multiple	operations	peak	pose
multiplication	opposite	pendant	positioned
multiplied	orators	penetration	positive
multiply(ing)	ordered	perceivable	possibility
mv	ordering	perceive	post
named	orders	percent	potential
nameplate	ordinance	perception	pour(ed)
nationally	ordinarily	perceptual	powerful
nearest	orientation	perform(s)	powers
necessarily	original	periodic(al)	practical(ly)
necessary	oscillator	permanent	practice
negative	otherwise	permeability	preapplied
negligence	ought	permissible	precaution
neoprene	outdoor	permit(s)	preceded
net(work)	outgrow	(ted*)	preceding
neutral	outlet*(s)	perpendicular	precise
nickel	outlined	personality	precision
nights	outlive	personally	precoated
nine	output	phase(s)	predict
nineteen	oven	pick	preliminary
ninety	overcome	pictorial	premounted
noisy	overcurrent	pin	prepaid
noncombustible	overhead	pipe(s)	prepare(d)
nonhazardous	overlapping	piping	prescribed
nonmagnetic	overload	places	presence
nonmetallic	owner	plain	presented
normally	oxygen	planned	presupposed
noted	oz.	plastic	prevent(s)
notice	pace	plate(s)	previous
numerous	page	platinum	primarily
nurseries	pain	played	primary
objection	paint	playing	principles
obtain	pair(s)	pleasant	printed
occupation	panel(s)	plug(ged)	prints
occupy	panelboard	plus	prior
occur(s)	papers	pointed	probability

Occupational Literacy Education

probe(s)
procedure
proceed
processes
produce(d)
  (s)
producing
product
profound
prohibited
project
proper(ly)
properties
protect(ed)
  (ion)
prove
provides
provision(s)
publicity
published
pull
pullboxes
pulse(s)
pump(s)
pure
purple
purposes
putting
quadratic
quantities
quantity
quarter
quickly
quit(s)
raceway(s)
radial
rags
rails
raised
ranges
rapidly
rare
rated
rating*(s)
ratio

reaches
react(ance)
readings
reality
realize
rearranged
reasonable
reasons
receive(r)
  (rs)
receptacle
recessed
recessing
reciprocal
recognize(d)
  (s)
recognizing
reconnected
reconnecting
recording
recovered
rectangular
rectified
rectifier
reduce(d)
reduction
reevaluating
refer(red)
  (s)
refrigerate
regard(less)
regular
regulate
regulation
rejection
relate(d)
  (s)
relative(ly)
relay*(s)
release
relieved
relocate
relocation
remain(s)
remedied

removal
remove(d)
rename
repaired
repairs
repeat(ed)
repelling
repetition
replace(d)
represent(ative)
  (ing) (s)
requested
require(ment)
reserved
reserves
reset
residual
resist(ance*)
  (ant) (or*) (ors)
resolve(d)
resolving
resonance
resonant
resources
respective
respects
respond(s)
responses
responsible
resultant
resulting
reused
revenge
reversal
reverse(s)
rigid
rise(r)
rocks
rolled
rolling
roofed
rooms
root(s)
rotated
rotates

rotating
rotation
rough(ing)
round
routed
row
rubber
rule(s)
runs
ruptured
safe(ty)
salesman
salvaged
samples
sap
satisfaction
satisfactory
satisfied
satisfy
saturated
Saturday
scale(d)
scare(d)
  (s)
scheduled
schematics
scientists
scratch
screen
screw(ed)
  (s)
seal(ed)
secondary
seconds
sections
secure(d)
security
seek(ing)
segments
seldom
select(ion)
self
self-concept
semiconductor
send(ing) (s)

senses
sensing
sensitivity
separate(d)
separating
separation
sets
setting
settle(d)
setup
seventy
severe
shafts
shakes
shaped
sharp
sheaths
shed
sheet
shipment
shock
shop
shortcircuit
shortest
shots
shovels
showing
shows
shunt
shut(s)(ting)
sign(s)
signal
significant
silver(s)
silverplate
similarly
simplex
simplified
simplify
simulates
simulating
simultaneous
site
sixteen(th)
 (ths)

sized
sizes*
sketch(es)
slide
slight(ly)
slot
smaller
smallest
smash
smell
smoke
snap(s)
sockets
soft
solenoid
solid
solution*(s)
solve(d)
solving
sounding
sounds
source(s)
southwest
spacers
spaces
specifically
specification*
specified*
spend
splice(s)
split
spot
square
stability
stable
stages
stainless
standards
standstill
starter
starts
stated
statements
staying
stays

steel
sticky
stimuli
stimulus
stopping
stops
storage
store
storeroom
stranded
stray
strengths
stressed
strictly
strips
strongly
structural
structure
stuck
studied
studies
stuff
subjected
submit
substance
substation
substitute
subtract(ed)
 (ion)
sufficient
suggestion
suitable
suites
sum
super
superintendent
supplement
supplied
supplies
supply(ing)
supported
supports
surge
surgical
survival

suspended
switch
switchboard
symbol
symmetrical
symmetry
synonymous
systematic
tags
takes
tall(er)
tank
tap(ped)
 (s)
task(s)
teams
technician
tedious
telephone
television
telling
tells
temporary
tend(s)
tent
term
terminal*(s*)
terminate(d)
terminating
termination
tested
testing
tests
text(books)
theories
therein
thermal
thermometer
thickness
thirteen
thirty
thoughtless
thousand*(th)
threats
throw(n) (s)

tile	unbroken	utility	watt(s)
tired	uncoated	utilization	wave(s)
tolerate	unconscious	utilize	(shape)
tolerating	underground	valve(s)	(shapes)
tool(s)	underneath	vapors	weak(ly)
torque	understood	variable(s)	wear
touch	underwriter	variation(s)	weather
tracings	uneven	variety	wet
trades	unfinished	vary(ing)	whenever
trailers	ungrounded	vast	wherever
train	uninsulated	ventilating	wherein
transformed	unique	verified	wider
transistor	unit(s)	verify	width
trapped	(y)	versus	winding(s)
treated	unknown*	vertical(ly)	windows
tremendous	(s)	vessels	wire*(d)
triangle(s)	unless	viewed	(s)
trig.	unnecessary	viscous	wiring*
triggered	unpleasant	visible	wise
trigonometry	unqualified	visually	withdrawal
trips	unsymmetric	volatile	wonder
trust	unused	volt*(age*)	workable
tub(s)	unusual	(ages*)	workmanlike
tube(s)	upper	(s*)	workmen
tubing	usable	voltmeter(s)	worse
tunnel(s)	usage	walls	wound
turning	useful	wants	wrapped
twenty	useless	warehouses	wreck
twice	uses	waste	yard
twist	u-shaped	watch(ing)	zero
unbalance	usual	waterproof	zinc

HIGH FREQUENCY WORDS
HEATING/AIR CONDITIONING MECHANIC

application	cycle	inches	relay
bottom	defrost	installed	resistance
branch	discharge	joint	safety
cabinet	drop	liquid	starting
cap	duct(s)	location	steel
capacity	electric(al)	manufacture	storage
check	energy	metal	suction
circuit	evaporator	models	supply
coil	expansion	mortar	switch
combination	feeder	oil	takeoff
compressor	fittings	operating	thermostat
condenser	flow	pipe	trunk
condensing	fluid	(s)	tubing
conditioning	foot	plenum	unit
connection	gas	pound	valve
constructing	gauge	proper	(s)
contract	glass	pump	velocity
controls	heat(ing)	refrigerant	voltage
cooling	ice	refrigerate	weight

TECHNICAL VOCABULARY
HEATING/AIR CONDITIONING MECHANIC

abnormally	amperage	basically	capable
absorbed	amperes	basin(s)	capacities
absorbing	amplifies	battery	capacitor
absorbs	angle	beam	capacity*
accepted	angular	bearing(s)	capillary
access(ible)	apart(ment)	bedded	capital
(ories) (ory)	apparatus	bedding	carbon
accomplish	appearance	belt	carry(ing)
accordance	application*	bend(s)	casing
accordingly	apply	bimetal	cast
accumulate	appreciable	bit(s)	catalog
accumulating	apprentice	blade	catalyst
accumulatory	approached	block(ed)	catch
accuracy	approaches	(ing)	caught
accurate(ly)	approaching	blow	caused
actions	appropriate	blower	causes
activates	approved	boil(er)	causing
acts	approximate	(ing)	cavitation
actual	arch	bolt(ed)	cement
actuated	Archimedes	bonds	centered
adapted	architect	border	centerline
adequate	arranged	bottom*	centers
adjacent	arrangement	bouyancy	certified
adjoining	article	bouyant	chalk
adjust(able)	asphalt	bracket(s)	chamber
(ed) (ment)	assemble(d)	branch*(es)	changed
advanced	assembly	break(s)	chapters
advantaged	assist(ance)	bronze	characteristic
advantages	assumed	btu(s)	charged
affect(ed)	assure	build(er) (s)	charging
(ing)	atmosphere	built	chart(s)
affords	attached	bulb	check*(ed)
agency	attempted	bulge	(out)
alarm	attract(ion)	bulk	chemical
alignment	automatic(ally)	burial	chisel
allowance	automobile	buried	circuit*(s)
allow(ed)	availability	burner(s)	classification
(s)	avoided	burning	cleared
alloy	backfill	butane	climates
alternate	backup	cabinet*(s)	coal
alternating	bacteria	cadmium	code(s)
alternator	balance	calculate(d)	coil*(s)
altitude	barely	calculation	collect
aluminized	base	cam	column
ambient	basement(s)	cap*	combination*

combined
combo
combustion
comfort(able)
comment
commercial
commonly
commutator
compact
companies
compared
competence
competent
competition
compiled
completed
complex(ity)
complicate
component(s)
compounds
compress(ed)
  (ing) (ion) (or*)
compromise
computation
computed
computing
concerning
concrete
condensate
condensating
condense(r*)
  (rs) (s)
condensing*
condition(ing*)
conductor
conform
connect(ed)
  (ing) (ion*)
conservation
considerable
consisting
constant
constructed
constructing*
consumption

contact(or)
  (s*)
contain(ed)
  (er) (ers) (s)
contaminate
content
continual
continues
continuous
contract(or)
contribute
contributing
controlled
controller
controlling
controls*
convenience
convention
conversion
convert
convex
convey(ed)
  (or)
cooler
cooling*
coolness
cools
coop
copper
correct(ly)
correspond
corrosion
counter
cradle
crankcase
crankshaft
collar
crew
critical
cross
crown
cube(s)
currents
curved
customer

cutout
cycle*(s)
cycling
cylinder
damage(d)
  (s)
damper(s)
danger(ously)
debris
decent
decrease(s)
decreasing
defective
defrost*
degrees
deliver(ed)
  (y)
deluxe
denser
densest
density
dependable
dependence
dependent
depending
depressed
describe(s)
description
designation
designer(s)
designing
desirable
desired
detail
determination
develop
device(s)
devise(s)
diagonal
diameter
die
differ(ed)
  (ent) (entiate)
diffuser
dilutes

dimension(s)
directed
directions
dirt(y)
disc
discharge*(d)
disconnect(ing)
discussed
discussing
displace(d)
  (ment) (s)
display
dissimilar
distances
distribute
distribution
distributor
disturb(ance)
dizziness
dock
domestic
downstairs
downward
drain
draw(ing)
  (ings) (n)
drop*(ped)
  (s)
dry
duct*(s*)
dynamically
economical
effectively
effectiveness
efficiency
eighths
electric*(al*)
  (ity)
electrode(s)
electromagnet
electron(ic)
element
elevation
eliminates
elsewhere

embedding
emersion
employing
employs
enamel
encased
encases
enclose
enclosure(s)
encounter
energized
energizes
energy*
engine
enter(ing)
    (s)
enthalpy
entrance
environment
equal(s)
equilibrium
equipped
equivalent
erosion
erratic
escape
essential
establish
estimate(d)
    (s)
estimating
etc.
ether
evaporate(d)
    (s)
evaporation
evaporative
evaporator*
eventually
exactly
examine
examples
exceed
excellent
exceptional

excerpt
excess(ive)
exchanger
exclusively
exerted
exerts
exhaust
exist(ing)
    (s)
expanding
expands
expansion*
expensive
experiment
exposed
exposure
extend(ed)
extension
external
extremely
factor(y)
failure
fairly
falls
false
fashioned
fastest
faucet
fault
features
feeder*
feeds
fiberglass
fig.
figured
filament
filings
filter(s)
fingers
fins
fireplace
firmly
fit(s) (ted)
    (ting) (tings*)
fixed

fixture(s)
flame
flange
flare
flaring
flash
flexible
floats
flow*(ing)
    (s)
flue
fluctuation
fluid*(s)
fluidic
flux
foam(ed)
foot*(ing)
forced
forest
forgot
formation
formed
formula
forth
fraction
frame
freely
freeze
freezing
frequently
friction
frost
frozen
ft.
fuel(s)
functioning
fundamental
furnace
furnish
    (ed)
fusible
fusion
gable
gain
gallon

gang
garage
gas*(eous)
    (es)
gasketing
gate
gauge*(s)
gear(ed)
generated
glass*
governed
gpm
grab(bed)
grade(s)
graph
gravity
grease
grille(s)
groove
grow
hammer
handle(d)
hanger
hardens
heat*(ed)
    (er) (ers) (ing*)
heavier
heavily
height
helical
hence
hiding
hinges
horizontal
horsepower
hose
houses
housing
hovered
humidity
hydraulic
ice*
icemaker
identify
ignition

illustration
immediately
immersed
impeller
impingement
imported
imposed
impossible
inch(es*)
included
incoming
incorrect
increases
independent
indicate(s)
indicative
inexhaustible
inferior
infiltrating
inherent
initial(ly)
initiated
initiating
inlet(s)
inner
inserted
inspected
install(ation)
  (ed) (er) (ing)
instance(s)
instruction
instructor
insufficient
insulating
insulation
insurance
insure
integral
intensity
interior
intermittant
intermitted
internal
interrupting
interrupts

intersection
invented
isolated
items
jackets
jar
jobs
joint*(s)
kinetic
kit(s)
latent
lavatory
layoff
layout
leader
leading
leak(age)
  (s)
leaving
lengthen(ing)
lengths
levels
lever
library
lift(ed)
  (s)
lightweight
limit(ing)
lineal
lined
linting
liquid*(s)
liquified
listed
listing
lists
lit
lites
liver
lives
load(ing)
locate(d)
locating
location*(s)
logical

louvers
lowered
lowering
lp
lubricated
machine(d)
  (s)
magnetic
mains
maintain(s)
manhole(s)
manifold
manual(ly)
manufacture*
marble
margin
mark(ing)
marketplace
match(ing)
materials
maximum
measure(d)
  (ment) (s)
measuring
mechanic(al)
medium
melt(ed)
  (s)
merchandise
metal*(s)
meter(ed)
  (ing)
metric
midair
milder
millivolts
minimum
minus
minute
missed
mistake
mixed
model(s*)
modification
modulate

modulating
moisture
met
mold
molecules
monitoring
monitors
mortar*
motion
motor(s)
mount(ed)
  (ing)
multi
multiple
multiplication
multiply(ing)
multispeed
needle
negative
nema
neutral
nipple
nominal
non
nonadjustable
nonpolluting
nonposition
normally
northeastern
object(s)
observed
obstruction
obtain(ing)
occasional
occupant
occur(red)
  (s)
offset(s)
ohms
oil*(s)
oneway
opening
operate(d)
operating*
operators

opposite	pipe*(s*)	progressive	reduction
optional	pipeline	promptly	reeds
ordered	piping	propane	refer(red)
orifice	piston(s)	proper*(ly)	refreezing
original	pitted	properties	refrigerant*
originate	planter	proportion	refrigerate*
OSHA	plaster	proposed	regained
outdoors	plastic	proprietor	region
outer	plate(s)	protect(ed)	register(ed)
outlet(s)	playing	(ing) (ion) (ors)	(s)
outlined	plenum*(s)	provides	regular
output	pliable	providing	regulates
overall	plug	provision	regulating
overcharge	plumb	psc	regulation
overcome	pneumatic	psi	regulator
overflow(s)	poisoning	psig	reinforced
overhead	polyurethane	ptc	related
overload(s)	porous	published	relations
overtime	port	puffing	relative(ly)
oxide	portion	pulley	relay*(s)
oxidized	positioning	pump*(ed)	release(d)
panel(s)	positive	(ing) (s)	remain(s)
parallel	potential	purchased	remodel
parcels	pound*(s)	quadrant	remote
partial(ly)	pour	quantities	remove(d)
partition(ed)	powered	quantity	removing
passing	practical	quarter	repair
patented	practice	ranging	repeated
path(s)	preceding	rapid(ly)	repel
pension	precise	rated	replacement
percentage	preheat	rating	represent(ed)
performance	prepared	reads	(ing) (s)
performs	preservation	reasonable	require(ment)
perimeter	preserves	recall	(s)
periodic	pressures	receiver	reservoir
periods	prevent(ing)	receives	reset
permanent	previously	receptacle	residence(s)
permit(s)	primarily	recirculate	residential
(ted) (ting)	principles	recognized	resistance*
pertinent	print(ing)	recommended	resistant
petroleum	procedure(s)	record(ed)	resisting
phase	processes	(ing) (s)	resists
physics	produce(d)	reduce(d)	respective
pieces	proficient	(r) (s)	responds
pilot	progresses	reducing	responsible

restriction
retainers
retains
retarded
returning
returns
reversed
reversing
review
ring(s)
rod(s)
roll(ed)
    (s)
roof
rooms
root
rose
rotor
rough
round
rubbing
rugged
rule(r)
    (s)
rumble
rumbling
runner
saddle
safety*
sanitary
satisfactory
satisfied
saturated
saturation
scaled
scope
seal(ed)
    (er)
seam
seasons
sections
securely
sedimentation
select(ed)
    (ion) (or)

sensation
sensiole
sensing
sensitive
separate(ly)
separation
servicing
settings
settle
shaft
shape(d)
sharp
sheet
shelf
shell
shielded
shipped
shipping
shortage
shortening
shows
shunts
shut
shutoff
shutters
sign
significant
silencer
simplify
sit
site
sizable
sized
sizes
sizing
slab
slanting
slick
slide
slightly
slings
slope(d)
slowing
smaller
smell

soil
solar
solder(ed)
solenoid
solid(ly)
solution
solving
soot
source(s)
spaces
specification
specified
speed
spigot
spoilage
spot
spout
squeaking
squeaky
stable
stack(s)
standing
standpoint
starter(s)
starting*
startup
stated
static
stationary
steam
steamfitted
steel*
stick(s)
stocked
stocking
storage*
store(d)
storeroom
storm
straighten
strainer
strains
straps
stream
structure(s)

style(s)
subcooler
submerged
substance(s)
subtract(ed)
    (ion)
succeeding
success
suction*
sufficient
suitable
summarize
sump
superfluous
superheat(ed)
superintendent
supplement
supplied
supplies
supply*(ing)
supported
supporting
supposed
surge
surplus
surrounding
suspension
sustains
switch*(ing)
tables
takeoff*(s)
tamped
tank
tap
technician
technique
tees
temporarily
tend(s)
tentatively
term(ed)
terminal(s)
termination
terrazzo
tested

tetrachloride	transmitted	upstream	volumes
textile	transported	upward	vulnerable
thermal	trap	usage	waist
thermistor	travel	utility	walls
thermocouple	trench	vacuum	wants
thermodynamic	trimmed	valuable	warmth
thermometer	trunk*	valve*(s)	washes
thermostat*	tube(s)	vane	washing
thick	tubing*	vapor(ization)	waste
thin	tunnel	(izes) (s)	waterproof
thoroughly	turbulence	variable(s)	weatherproof
thrust	turbulent	variation	weighed
tin	turning	varies	weight*(ed)
tissue	typical	vary	(less)
tolerate	UG	vault	(s)
tools	uncluttered	velocities	wick
torque	underground	velocity*	width
totals	undisturbed	vent(ilating)	winding
touch(ing)	unevenness	(ilation)	winter
tower(s)	uniform	vertical(ly)	wire(d)
traffic	unit*(s)	vessel(s)	(s)
trailer	universal	vibrating	wiring
trains	unknown	vinyl	worksheet
transfer(red)	unless	viscosity	wrap
(ring)	unlike	vitrified	yard
transformed	unnecessary	voids	yearly
transition	unopened	volt(age*)	yeast
transmission	upper	(s)	zero

HIGH FREQUENCY WORDS
INDUSTRIAL MAINTENANCE MECHANIC

air	diameter	meter	refrigeration
angle	differential	minimum	relay
application	discharge	motor	relief
approximate	discs	mounted	resistance
braking	electrical	occur	resistor
cap	element	ohm	reverse
causes	energy	oil	screws
centrifugal	evaporator	operate	seal
chamber	factory	operating	setting
check	float	opposite	source
circuit	flow	output	speed
compressor	fluid	pan	stroke
condenser	formula	pilot	suction
connected	gas	pipe	supply
connection	gauge	piston	switch
contacts	heat	port	tank
controller	hydraulic	prevent	teeth
deflection	lift	proper	thousand
degrees	liquid	psi	valve(s)
determined	maximum	pump	volt(age)
device	mechanical	refrigerant	wear

TECHNICAL VOCABULARY
INDUSTRIAL MAINTENANCE MECHANIC

abbreviate
ability
abnormal
abrasive
absorbed
absorbing
absorbs
abuse
ac
accelerate
acceleration
acceptable
accepted
accessible
accessories
accessory
accommodate
accompanying
accomplished
accordingly
accumulate(d)
accumulation
accuracy
accurate(ly)
achieve
acid
acting
activates
acts
actual
actuates
actuating
actuator(s)
acute
adapted
add(ing)
(s)
addendum
adequate
adjacent
adjust(able)
(ed) (ing) (ment)
advanced
advantage(d)
(s)

affect(ed)
affords
agency
agent
air*
alarm
algebraic
align(ed)
(ing) (ment)
allow(able
(ed) (ing) (s)
alloy(ing)
(s)
alternate(d)
aluminum
ambient
amounts
amp(erage)
ampere(s)
amplifies
anchored
angle*(s)
angular
anomaly
antifreeze
antimony
anybody
anyway
anywhere
apart
apparatus
appearance
appliance(s)
application*
applies
apply(ing)
appreciable
apprentice
approached
approaches
approval
approved
approximate
arbitrarily
arbitrary

arch
arcing
arise
arithmetic
arm(ature)
arranged
arrival
article
artificial
assemble
assembly
assigned
assist(ance)
associated
assume
assure(d)
atmosphere
atmospheric
atoms
attach(ed)
(ing) (ment)
attempted
attract(ion)
auto(matic)
(matically)
automobile
automotive
availability
avoid
axis
bacteria
bands
bar
bare
barium
base(s)
baseplate
basically
battery
battle
beam
bearing(s)
becomes
begin(s)
belongs

bend(er)
(s)
beneficial
bias
bimetal
bipolar
bismuth
bit
bite
blade
blank
bleed
block(ed)
(ing) (s)
blow(er)
(ing) (n)
blueprints
boil(er)
(s)
bolts
bonds
books
bore(d)
boring
bottle
bottom
bounce
bowl
box(es)
bracket(s)
brake(s)
braking*
branch
brass
break(down)
(er) (ers)
bridge
broken
brush(es)
btu(s)
bubbles
bucket
buffing
builds
buildup

built
bulb
bullet(ing)
(ins)
bullneck
burial
burn(ed)
burrs
bushings
butane
button
bypass
cabinet
cadmium
cage
calcium
calculate(d)
calculating
calculation
calibrated
calls
cam
canister
canvas
cap*
capacities
capacitive
capacitor
capacity
carbon
carefully
carrier(s)
carry(ing)
casing
cast(ing)
catalyst
catch
caused
causes*
causing
caution
cavities
cemented
centerline
centrifugal*

centrifuge
cents
chamber*
chances
changed
changing
chapters
characteristic
charged
charges
charging
chart
check*(ed)
chemical(s)
cherry
chilled
chromium
circle
circuit*(s)
circular
circumference
clamped
clamps
clarified
classes
classification
classified
clean(ing)
clearance
climates
climb
clock(wise)
closely
closes(t)
closing
cloth
cloudy
coal
coarse(r)
coat
cobalt
code(s)
coil(ed)
(s)
coke

collect(or)
(s)
colored
column
combination
combustible
combustion
comfort
commonly
communicate
commutator
compact
comparative
compared
compartment
compensate
compensatory
competence
competition
compiled
complaint
completed
completes
complex
component(s)
composition
compound
compress(ed)
(ion) (or*)
comprise
computed
concerning
condensate
condensation
condense(r*)
(s)
condition(ing)
conduct(ion)
(or)
conduit
cone
conjunction
connect(ed*) (s)
(ing) (ion*) (or)
consequent

considerable
considerate
consists
constants
construction
consult(ing)
consumption
contact(ed)
(or) (ors) (s*)
contain(ed)
(er) (ment) (s)
contamination
content
continues
continuous
contour(ed)
contribution
controlled
controller*
controlling
controls
convenience
convenient
convention
convert(ed)
conveyer
cool(ed)
(est) (ing) (s)
copper
core
corners
correct(ed)
correlation
correspond
corrode
corrosion
cotton
counted
counter
coupled
coupler
coupling
cover(ing)
(s)
crack(ed) (s)

crankcase	describe(s)	disruptive	electric(al*)
crankshaft	descriptive	dissimilar	(ian) (ity)
creates	designated	distorts	electromagnet
crescent	designing	distribute	electron(ic)
critical	desk(s)	divided	(s)
cross	destroy	dividing	element* (ary)
crystal	detailed	domestic	elevators
cube(s)	detection	doors	eliminate(d)
cubic	deteriorate	dotted	(s)
curie	determined*	downstream	eliminating
currently	develop(s)	downtime	embedding
currents	devented	dozed	emergency
cursor	device*(s)	dozen	emersion
curvature	devise(d)	drag	emery
cushion(s)	(s)	drain(ed)	employ(ed)
cutaway	diagram(s)	(s)	(s)
cuts	dial(s)	draw(ing)	encases
cutter(s)	diameter*(s)	(ings) (n)	enclosed
cutterhead	diametrical	drawbar	enclosure(s)
cycle(s)	diaphragm	drift	encountered
cylinder(s)	die	drilled	ends
damage(d)	dielectric	drink	endwise
damper(s)	differential*	drip	energize(d)
dart	difficulties	driven	(s)
datum	digit	driver(s)	energy*
dc	dilemma	drives	engineers
deadman	dilutes	driving	enlargement
decrease(s)	dimensions	drop(out)	ensure
decreasing	dinner	(ped) (s)	enter(ing)
defective	directed	drum	(s)
defined	directional	dry	enthalpy
definite	directions	duct	entirely
deflection*	dirt(y)	dull	equal(ly)
defrost(ed)	disadvantage	dump(s)	(s)
degrees*	disagree	dust(s)	equations
delay	disassemble	duty	equilibrium
delivery	disc(s*)	ease	equipped
demand	discharge*	eccentricity	equivalent
densities	disconnect	economical	erection
density	discussed	edge(s)	erratic
depend(ence)	discussing	effectively	escape
(ent) (ing) (s)	disintegrate	effectiveness	essential
depress(ed)	dispenser	efficiency	(ly)
(es)	displacement	efficient	established
depth	display	elbow	etc.

evaporated	faulty	forged	gets
evaporating	feature	forks	girders
evaporator*	fed	formation	giving
exact(ly)	feedback	formula*(s)	gland
examine	feeder	forth	glass
examples	feeding	forty-five	glue(d)
exceed	ferrous	fourth(s)	gluing
exception(al)	fiberglass	fractional	goes
excerpt(s)	fields	frame	gold
excess(ive)	fig.	freely	governing
(ively)	figured	freerunning	gpm
excuse	filament	freezing	grade(s)
exercised	fill(ed)	freight	gradual(ly)
exerted	(ers) (ing) (s)	frequency	graduated
exhausted	filter(ed)	frequently	graduation
exists	finding	friction	grain(less)
expands	finer	frost(ing)	graphic
expansion	fingers	frounds	gravity
expedite	finish(ing)	frozen	grease(s)
expense	fit(s)	ft.	grip
expensive	(ting) (tings)	fuel(s)	grooves
experiment	fixed	full(y)	grounded
explained	flame	functions	grounding
explosion	flammable	fundamental	grow
explosive	flare	funnel	guess
exposed	flaring	furnace	guidebar
exposure	flash	furnished	guidelines
expressed	flask	furthermore	guy(s)
expression	flat(tening)	fuse(s)	hack
extension	flavor	fusion	halves
extensively	flexible	gage(s)	hammer
external(ly)	flight	gal.	handle(s)
extra	float*	galling	handling
extreme(ly)	flooded	gallons	happen(s)
facing	flour	gas*(eous)	hardened
factor(y*)	flow*(ing)	(es)	hardens
facts	(s)	gasket(ing)	harmful
failure(s)	fluctuation	gauge*	harsh
fairly	fluid*(ic)	gear	harvest(ed)
falls	flux	generate(d)	hazardous
familiar	flywheel	(s)	heads
fan	foam(ed)	generating	heat*(ed)
fashioned	follows	generation	(er) (ers) (ing)
faster	foot	generator	heavily
fattened	forced	geographic	helical

hence	index	isolated	lights
hide	indicate(s)	isolating	limits
highly	indicating	isolation	link(age)
hinges	indicative	items	liquid*(s)
hiring	indicator	jobs	liquified
hits	indirect	joints	listed
holders	indoors	keeps	listen
holding	inductive	kilo	listing
holds	inefficient	kilogram	lists
hole(s)	inertia	kinetic	lit
hollows	inexhaustible	knocks	lithium
hook(s)	inexpensive	knuckles	load(ed)
hopefully	infinite	labels	(ing) (s)
horizontal	initial(ly)	ladder	locate(d)
horsepower	initiated	lags	locating
housing	initiating	laid	location(s)
hubs	inlet	lamp	locker
humidifier	inner	lapse	locknut
humidistat	input	largest	locomotive
humidity	insert(ed)	latent	logarithms
hundredth	inspect(ed)	lathe	logical
hydraulic*	(ing) (ion)	latitude	loop
I-beam	install(ation)	lattice	loosely
ice	(ed) (ing)	layers	loosen
ideal	instance	laying	loses
idler	instruction	lbs.	loss
illustrate	instrument	leader	lowered
illustration	insufficient	leading	lowering
immediately	insulation	leads	lowest
immovable	insulator	leak(age)	lubricant
impedance	insure	(ing) (s)	lubricated
impeller	integral(ly)	lean	lubricating
imported	intended	leaving	lubrication
impractical	intense	lefthand	lucky
impregnate	intensity	leg	machinable
improper	interdependent	lengthen(ing)	machine(d)
inch(es)	interfere	lengths	(s)
(ing)	internal	lengthwise	magnesium
includes	interrupts	levels	magnet(ic)
incoming	intimate	lever	(ism) (ized)
incorrectly	inverted	lies	(izing)
increases	invisible	lift*(ed)	maintain(ed)
increasing	involving	(ing)	(ing)
increment(s)	inward	lighter	maintenance
independent	iron	lightest	majority

manganese
manifold
manometer
manual(ly)
manufacture
mark(ings)
  (s)
marketplace
master
match
mate
materials
mating
maximum
measure(d)
  (ment) (s)
measuring
mechanical*
meets
melt(ed)
memory
merchandise
mercury
mesh(es)
messed
metal(s)
meter*(ed)
  (ing) (s)
metric
microampere
micrometer
microsecond
milder
milliliter
millimeter
millivolts
mills
mine(s)
mineral
minimizes
minimum*
minority
minus
minute
misalignment

mistuned
mixed
mixture(s)
mode
model(s)
moderate
modification
modulate
modulating
moisture
mold
molecular
molecules
monitoring
monitors
monthly
motion
motors
mounted*
mounting
mover
multiple
multiplication
multiply(ing)
multipurpose
needle
negative
neighborhood
net
network
neutral
nickel
nicks
ninety
nipple
nitrogen
nominal
nonfoaming
nonmagnetic
nonpolluting
nonposition
normally
northeastern
notations
nozzle

numeral(s)
nuts
oak
object(ive)
obtain(ing)
occur*(s)
ohm*(meter)
  (s)
oil*(s)
opening
opens
operate*(d)
  (s)
operating
operative
operator
opposed
opposite*
optional
ordering
ordinary
orifice
original
originating
oscillator
outdoor(s)
outer
outlet(s)
output*
outward
overcome
overflow
overheating
overload
override
oxidation
oxide
packaged
packings
page
painted
pair
pan*(s)
paragraph(s)
parallel(ing)

part time
partial(ly)
partition
pass(age)
  (es) (ing)
path(s)
peak(s)
pedal
percent(age)
perform(ing)
  (s)
periodic(al)
periods
periphery
permanent
permeability
permit(s)
  (ting)
personnel
petroleum
phase(s)
phlange
physics
pick(ed)
pictorial
pieces
pilot*(ed)
pin(s)
pinion
pipe*(d)
  (s)
piping
piston*(s)
pit(ting)
pitch(es)
placing
plants
plaster
plate(s)
platinum
plug(ged)
plumb
plus
pneumatic
pocket

pointed
pointing
polarities
polarity
polishing
polyurethane
pop(s)
port*
portion
position(ed)
  (ing) (s)
positive
possibly
post
potential
pound(s)
pour
powered
powers
practical(ly)
practice(s)
precise
precision
predetermined
predominant
preheat
premature
premium
presents
preservation
preserves
preset
pressures
pressurize
prevent*(ative)
  (ing)
previous(ly)
prices
primary
prime(r)
principally
principles
printed
printing
prior

procedures
proceed
processes
produce(d)
  (s)
producing
product
proficient
programed
prompt
proof
propane
proper*(ly)
properties
proportion
protect(ed)
  (ing)
providing
psc
psi*
ptc
pull(ed)
  (ey) (s)
pulsating
pulse(s)
pump*(ed)
  (ing) (s)
punched
purposes
pushed
pushing
putting
quantities
quantity
quarter
quickly
races
rack
radial(ly)
radius
raise(d)
raising
ram
ranges
rapidity

rapidly
rare
rated
rating(s)
ratio
reaches
reaching
reactance
readily
readjust
reads
rearranged
receive(r)
  (ers) (s)
receptacle
recharging
reciprocal
reciprocate
recirculate
recognized
recommend
  (ation)
  (ed)
recording
recovered
rectangular
reduce(d)
  (s)
reduction
reeds
refer(red)
refined
refineries
refreezing
refrigerant*
refrigeration*
regained
regardless
region
regular
regulates
regulation
regulator
relationship
relative(ly)

relay*(s)
release(d)
  (s)
reliability
relief*
relieve
remain(s)
remedied
remote(ly)
removal
remove(d)
removing
repair
repeat(ed)
repel(ling)
repetition
replace(d)
  (ment)
replacing
reporting
reposition
represent(s)
reproduced
reproduction
require(ment)
  (s)
reservoir
reset
resin
resistance*
resistant
resisting
resistor*(s)
resonance
resonant
respective
responds
restore
restraining
restricted
resultant
resulting
retains
retard(ed)
retraction

returning
returns
reverse*(d)
  (s)
review
revolution
ribs
rifle
right
rigid
rim
ring
rise(s)
rising
rod(s)
rollers
rooms
root(s)
rotary
rotate(d)
  (s)
rotating
rotation
rotor
rough
round(ed)
row
rubber
rugged
rule(s)
runner
runs
rust
saddle
safe(ty)
sag
sand
sandwich
satisfactory
satisfied
saturated
saturation
saving
scale(d)
  (s)

scheduled
scoring
scratch(es)
screw(ing)
  (s*)
seal*(ing)
  (s)
seasons
seating
seats
seconds
sectional
sections
secure(d)
securing
seldom
selected
selecting
selection
self
selling
semiconduct
sends
sensed
senses
sensing
sensitivity
separate(ly)
separation
sequence(d)
serial
serviceability
servicing
setting*(s)
setup
severe
severity
sewed
sewing
shaft(s)
shape
sharp(ness)
sheet
shift(ing)
shiny

shipment
shipped
shock
shoe(s)
shop
shortage
shortening
shorter
shortest
shows
shunts
shut(s)
shutdown
sides
sight
signal
significant
signs
silver(s)
similarly
simultaneously
sitting
sizes
sizing
sleeve
slide
sliderule(s)
slight(ly)
slot(s)
slow(ing)
slurries
slurry
smaller
smooth
soap(s)
sockets
sodium
soft
solar
sold
solder(ed)
solenoid
solid(s)
solution
solve

source*
spaces
span
specialist
specialize
specially
specifically
specification
specified
speed*(s)
spend
spin
spindles
spoilage
spool
spot(s)
springload
springs
sprung
spur
stability
stable
stages
stainless
stalled
standing
standpoint
starch
starting
starts
starve
stated
stations
staying
stays
steam
steel(s)
steep
stem(s)
stick(ing)
stiff
stopping
stops
storage
store(d)

storeroom
straighten
strain(er)
(s)
stray
stream
stressed
string
strips
stroke*
stronger
strongly
strontium
structural
structure
stub
stuck
stuff
style
subcooling
subjected
substance(s)
substantial
suction*
sufficient
suitable
sum
sump
super
superheat
superheated
supplied
supply*(ing)
supported
supports
supposed
surfaces
surge
surgical
surrounding
suspended
suspension
switch*(ed)
(es) (ing)
symbols

symmetrical
symmetry
syphon(ing)
tables
tags
takes
tangent
tank*
tanned
tape
taper(ing)
(s)
taperheaded
taps
task
technically
technician
technique
technological
tee
teeth*
temp.
temporarily
temporary
tend(ency)
tension
tenth
term
terminal(s)
terminated
text
textile
theoretical
thereby
thermal
thermistor
thermodynamic
thermometer
thermostat
thick(ness)
thin
thorough(ly)
thousand*(th)
thread(ed)
(s)

throat
through
throw
tight(ly)
tighten(ing)
till
timed
tolerances
tool(s)
tooth
torque
touch
toward
trained
transfer(red)
transform(ed)
(ing)
transistor
transition
transmission
transmitted
transported
travel(ing)
tray
treated
triggered
trigonometry
trimmed
tripped
trips
truck
tube(s)
tubing
turning
turns
twenty
twice
twirled
twisted
twisting
u-shaped
ultimately
unassemble
unbalanced
undercut(ting)

underneath
underside
understood
underwrite
unequal
unidirectional
uniform
unit(s)
(y)
universal
unknown
unless
unlike
unload(ed)
unmodified
unsymmetrical
unwanted
upper
upright
upside
upward
usage
useful
user
usual
utilized
vacuum
valuable
valve*(s*)
vane(s)
vapor(ization)
(izes) (izing) (s)
variable
variation(s)
varied
vary(ing)
velocity
vent(s)
vertical(ly)
vibrating
viewing
vinyl
viscosity
visually
volatile

volt*(s)
voltmeter(s)
wait
walls
warm(th)
washers
washes
wasted
watch
waterproof
wave(s)
waveshape(s)

weak(ly)
wear*
wedging
weight(ed)
(less)
welcome
wet
wheel(s)
whereas
wick
widely
wider

width
winding
(s)
wings
wipe(r)
wiping
wire(d)
(s)
wood
(en)
wool
workmen

worm
wormgear
wormwheel
worn
wrapped
wrench
wrinkling
yearly
yeast
zero
zinc
zone

HIGH FREQUENCY WORDS
LICENSED PRACTICAL NURSE

administer	disease	mouth	physician
bath	(s)	muscle	procedure
bit	dry	(s)	proper
blanket	ear	nasal	site
brain	external	needle	skin
catheter	female	nurse	stomach
cells	fluid	ordered	thank
chair	glands	orders	tissue
check	infection	pain	traction
clean	juice	patient	tube
condition	medication	(s)	unit

abbreviate
abdomen
abdominal
abilities
ability
abnormal(ity)
abortion(s)
abscess
absolutely
absorbed
absorption
accept(able)
    (ance) (ed) (ing)
access(ory)
accident(al)
    (s)
accommodating
accompanies
accompany
accomplish
accounted
accredited
accumulating
accurate
achieve(d)
acidic
acidosis
acids
acoustic
acquire
acted
actions
active
acts
actual
acute
add(ing) (itive)
    (itives) (s)
adeno
adequate(ly)
adhere
adhesive
adjacent
adjoining
adjust(ment)

administer*
admission
admit(ting)
adrenal
adult(s)
advance
advantage(s)
adverse
advise
aerosol
affect(ed)
    (ing)
    (ion)
affiliated
affix
afraid
aged
agencies
agency
agent(s)
ages
agitation
agree
aids
airway
alcohol(ism)
alert
algia
aligned
alignment
alimentary
alkaline
allergen(s)
allergic
allergy
allow(ed)
    (s)
alter
altogether
alveolar
alveoli
ambulate
ambulating
ameliorating
amino

amounts
ampule
anal
analgesic
analyze(r)
anatomical
anchor(ed)
    (ing)
ancient
anemia
anesthesia
anesthetic
aneurysm
angiograph
angle
ankle
annually
anorexia
answers
antepartum
anterior(ly)
anthologic
antiabortion
antibiotic
antibodies
anticipate
anticoagulant
antiseptic
anus
anvil
anxiety
anybody
anything*
aortic
appearance
appears
appended
appliance(s)
application
apply(ing)
appropriate
approximate
aquamatic
aqueous
argue

arises
arm(ed)
armchair
armlets
arranged
arrangement
arranges
arrhythmia
arrives
arterial
arteries
arteriosclerosis
artery
articles
artificial
ascending
aseptic
aside
aspects
aspirin
assemble
assess(ment)
assigned
assist(ance)
    (ing) (s)
assume(s)
assuming
assurance
assure(d)
atheist(s)
atmosphere
atria
atrophy
attach(ed)
attend(ance)
attitudes
auditory
automatic(ian)
avoid(ed)
    (s)
awake(n)
aware
axial
axilla
axillary

axis	bit*	button	cerebral
baby	bladder	cabinet(s)	ceremony
bacteria(l)	blanket*(s)	caking	cervical
bacteriostasis	bleed(ing)	calibration	cervix
balance(d)	blinking	calorie	chair*(s)
band	bloodletting	canal(s)	challenge(d)
bank	bloodstream	cancels	chamber
baptism	blurry	cancer	changed
bar(s)	board(s)	cannula(s)	changing
bare(ly)	bodies	cans	chapel
barrel	bodily	canvas	chapter(s)
base	bone(s)	cap	characteristics
basically	bottle(s)	capable	charged
basin	bottom	capacity	charges
bath*(s)	bowel	capillaries	charging
bathe	brace(s)	capsule	chart(ing)
bathing	brachial	carbohydrate	check*(ed)
bathroom	braid(ed)	carbon	(ing)
beat(s)	(ing) (s)	carcinoma	cheek
bedding	brain*	card	chemical
bedmaking	break	cardiac	chemosensis
bedpan	breakdown	cardiovascular	chemotherapy
beds	breakfast	cared	chest
bedside	breast	careful(ly)	chilling
behave	breath	caring	chocolate
behavior	breathe	carotid	choking
belief(s)	bridgework	carrier	chronic(ally)
believed	bringing	carry(ing)	chronological
bell	brings	cart(s)	churned
belly	broken	cartilaging	cigarette
bend	bronchi	cast	cilia
beneficial	(als)	catch(ing)	circle(s)
benefit	(oles)	catheter*(ize)	circuits
benign	bruise	caught	circular
bent	brush	caused	circulation
benzine	bubbles	causes	circulator
besides	bubbling	causing	circumstance
betaine	buckets	caution	circumvent
bevel	build	cavities	cirrhosis
bile	built	cavity	cisternal
billionths	bundles	cease	civilized
bills	burned	ceiling	claims
bin	burning	cells*	clamp
biopsy	burns	cellular	classified
birth	buttocks	centers	clean*(ed) (ing)

cleanliness
cleanse
clears
clergy(man)
cling
clinical
clockwise
closely
closer
closets
closeup
clothes
clothing
clubfoot
clues
clumping
cluster(s)
cochlea
code
collapse
collar
collateral
collection
colon
colored
colors
colostomies
colostomy
column
coma(tose)
comb(ed)
combat
combination
combine(d)
combining
comfort(able)
commands
commercial
commode
commonly
communicate
communion
comparison
complain(ed)
complement

completed
complex(ity)
complicate
complication
component(s)
composed
compress(ion)
concentrate
concept(ion)
   (s)
concern(ing)
   (s)
condition*
conducive
conduction
cones
confined
confirmation
conform
confused
congenital
congestion
conjunction
conjunctive
connect(ed)
   (ing) (ion) (s)
conscious(ness)
consent(ed)
   (s)
consequently
considerate
consist(s)
constant(ly)
constipate
constipation
contain(er)
   (ing) (s)
contaminate
content
contest
continues
continuing
continuous
contract(ed)
   (ion)

contraindicate
contrast
contribute
contributing
controlled
controlling
controls
convenience
convenient
cooled
cooling
cools
coordination
cope
cord(s)
cornea
corners
correct(able)
   (ive)
   (ly)
correlation
corridor(s)
corset(s)
cotton
cough(ing)
counseling
counselor
count
coupled
courts
cover(ing)
   (s)
cradle
cranial
cranium
cream
credit
crest
crimping
crippled
crippling
crisis
critical
crooked
cross

croupette
crowded
crusting
crusts
cup(s)
curable
cure
curved
cutdown
cute
cuts
cycle
cyst(s)
damage(d)
danger(ous)
date(d)
deafness
dealing
dealt
decides
decrease(d)
deems
deeper
defacation
defatting
deficiency
deficient
defining
definite(ly)
definition
deformities
defrost
degrees
dehydration
delay(ed)
delivery
deltoid
demanding
demands
demonstrate
dentures
depend(ency)
   (ent) (ing) (s)
deposited
depress(ed) (ion)

depth
derivative
dermis
descending
designated
desirable
desire(d)
(s)
desirous
destitute
destroy(ed)
destruction
detail(s)
detect(ing)
develop(ing)
(s)
deviation
devices
diabetes
diabetic
diagnose(d)
diagnosis
dial
diarrhea
diastole
die
diet
dietary
differ
difficulties
diffusion
digest(ion)
(ive)
dilated
diluent
dim
dimples
dinner
dioxide
diphtheria
directed
directing
directions
directives
directs

dirty
disabilities
disbelieve
discard
discharge(d)
discomfort
discontinuous
discourage
discovery
discussed
discussing
discussion(s)
disease*(s*)
disinfect
disintegrate
disks
disorder(s)
displays
disposable
dispose
distended
distends
distilled
distinguish
distortion
disturbance
divide(d)
dividing
doctor(s)
dormant
dosage
doses
downward
drag
drainage
draining
drains
drastic
draw
drawer
drawsheet
dressing
dried
drink(s)
drip

drop(ped)
(s)
drug(s)
drum
dry*
ducts
duties
duty
dying
dyscrasia
ear*(s)
eardrum
earliest
ease
easier
eat(en)
(ing)
edge
effectively
eggs
eight(h)
(y)
elapses
elasticity
elderly
elective
electrical
electrocardiogram
electrolyte
electronic
element
elevated
elevation
elevator(s)
eleven
eliminate
elimination
embryo
emergencies
emergency
emotion(al)
empathy
emphysema
employed
emptied

empty
enabled
enables
encased
enclosing
encounter
encourage(s)
ending
endocrine
endometriosis
endometrium
endoplasmic
enema(s)
energy
engulf
enlarged
ensues
ensure
enter(ed)
(ing) (s)
enterobius
entirely
entitled
entrances
entwining
envelope
environment
enzyme(s)
epidermis
epiglottis
epilepsy
epimysium
epithelial
equal
(ized)
(ly)
equinovarum
equipped
era
errand
error
erythema
escape(s)
esophageal
esophagus

essential(s)
estimates
etc.
ethical
ethmoid
eustachian
evacuate
evaluate
evaluation
evasive
event
exact(ly)
examination
examined
examples
exceeds
excess(ive)
excreta
excretory
excuse
exercise
exerted
exhibits
exist(ing)
exit(ing)
    (s)
exocrine
expiration
explain
explanation
expose(d)
    (s)
exposing
expressed
extend(ed)
    (ing) (s)
extension
extra
extreme(ly)
extremities
faces
facial
facilitate
facility
factor(y)

failure(s)
fairly
falls
false
familial
familiar
families
fast
fasten(ed)
    (s)
fat
fearful
fed
feeding
feelings
feels
female*
femoral
fetal
fetus
fever
fibers
fibrotic
fibrous
fifth
fifty
fill(ed)
    (er) (ing)
filter(ing)
financial
finding
finish(ed)
finite
firmly
firmness
first aid
fishworm
fist
fit(s)
fix
    (ed)
flakes
flash
flat(tens)
flatus

flexed
flexible
floors
flow
fluid*(s)
flush(ed)
fly
focal
focus
fold(ed)
    (s)
folks
follicles
follow(s)
foods
footboard
forced
forcing
forgot
formal
formation
formulas
forth
fortunately
forty
fosters
foundation
fracture(s)
frame
framework
frank
freely
freeze
freezing
frequency
frequent(ly)
frustration
fulcrum
functional
functioning
functions
fundamental
fungi
furnishing
fusses

gain(ing)
gallbladder
gases
gauze
generalize
generated
generation
genetic(ally)
genital(s)
gentle
gently
germicidal
girth
giving
gland(s*)
glass
glove
glucose
gluteal
glycerol
goals
gonococcus
gonorrhea
goodness
gown
gradual
graduate
gram
grandparent
grapefruit
graphs
gravity
greatest
greatly
greenish
grounds
groupings
grow(n)
guard
guide
guideline(s)
gurgling
habits
halter
hammer

hamper	hygiene	infant(s)	internal
handle	hyper	infarction	interpersonal
hang(s)	hyperalimentation	infect(ed)	interpret
harmony	hyperextend	infection*(s)	interrelation
hasten	hypersensis	(ious)	interruption
hazardous	hyphen	infective	intervals
hazards	hypothalamus	infestation	intervertebral
headache	hysterectomy	inflammation	interview
heal(ing)	IV	inflammatory	intestinal
hearing	ice(d)	inflow	intestine
heat(ed)	identify	influenced	intolerance
heavily	iliac	inform(ed)	intrauterine
heel	ilium	infraction	intravenous
helped	ill	infusion(s)	introduce(d)
helpful	illegal	ingested	introduction
helping	illness(es)	inhabit	introductory
helps	illustrate	inhibit(s)	invade(s)
hemolytic	imbalance	initial(ly)	invasion
hemorrhage	immediately	initiate(d)	invention
hemothorax	immobilize	initiative	inventory
hence	immunization	inject(ed)	involve(ment)
hereditary	impaired	(ion) (s)	(s)
highly	impending	injuries	involving
hinder	implies	injury	inward
hip(s)	improper	inner	iris
holder	improve(s)	insert(ed)	irregular
holding	improving	(ion)	irreligious
holes	impulses	inspect	irrigation
holidays	incapable	inspiration	irritable
homemakers	inch(es)	inspired	irritating
hopper	incident	instant	irritation
horizontal	incise	instituted	itching
hormone(s)	incision	institution	item
hose	included	instruct(ion)	jams
hospitable	includes	(or)	jaw
hospitalize	incoming	instrument	jeopardize
hospitals	incompatible	insulin	joins
host	increases	insure	joint(s)
housekeeping	increasing	intact	judgment
humidity	independent	intake	juice*(s)
hundreds	index	intent	jump(ing)
hungry	indicate	interfere(nce)	keeping
hurried	indicating	(s)	key(s)
hurt(ing)	indication	interior	kidneys
(s)	induces	interlacing	kilo

kin
kinds
knee
knitting
knob
knowledgeable
lab
labeled
laboratory
laboring
lace
lacrimation
lag
laid
lanolin
lap
largely
larynx
latent
lateral(is)
  (ly)
laundry
laws
laxatives
layer(s)
leader
leading
leads
leeches
leg
legal(ized)
legislature
legs
lengths
lengthwise
lesions
lessons
lets
letting
levels
lever(s)
licensed
licensure
lifesaving
lift(s)

ligaments
lightest
lightning
lights
limb
limiting
limits
lined
linen(s)
lining
linked
linking
liquid(s)
liver
lobe(s)
localized
locate(d)
location
lock(ed)
  (ing) (s)
locomotion
lodged
longterm
loneliness
loose(ly) (n)
lose
losing
loss
lotion
loud
LPN
lubricant
lubricate
lubrication
lues
lumbar
lumbosacral
lumen
lump
lung(s)
lymph
lysis
machine
maintain(ed)
  (ing) (s)

maintenance
maker
male
maleus
malignancy
malignant
malnourish
malnutrition
malunion
manage(d)
manifest(ation)
  (ed)
mankind
manual
mark(ed)
marriage
masceration
massage
mastectomy
master
mastoiditis
mate
materials
matted
mattress
mature
maxilla
maximum
meals
meanings
meantime
meanwhile
measure(d)
  (s)
measurement(s)
measuring
meatus
mechanical
mechanics
mechanism
media
medically
medicated
medication*
medicine

medium
medulla
membrane(s)
meningeal
meningitis
menstrual
menstruation
mental
messages
metabolic
metabolism
metal
meter
micro
microorganism
microphone
microscope
microscopic
mild
mineral(s)
minimal
minimum
minister(s)
mino
minute
misc.
mitochondria
mix(ed)
mobility
moderate
modification
moist(ening)
  (ens)
  (ure)
molecules
monitoring
mopping
motion
motor
mouth*
movements
mucosa
mucuous
multiply
muscle*(s*)

muscular	obstetrical	oxygen(ation)	Persistalis
muslin	obstruct(ed)	pace	personality
myasthenia	(ion)	packet	personnel
myocardial	obtain(ing)	pain*(ful)	perspiration
mysteries	obvious	palate	persuasion
narcosis	occipital	palpate	pertaining
narcotic(s)	occupies	palpation	phagocytes
nasal*	occur(s)	pancreas	pharmacology
nationally	o'clock	pancreatic	pharmacy
nausea	ocular	panel	pharynx
neck	offer(ed)	pap	phase
needle*	official(s)	paralysis	philosophy
neglect(ed)	offspring	paralyzed	phonation
neonatal	oil(s)	parasitic	physically
neurotic	ointment	Parkinson's	physician*(s)
nodes	olfactory	partial	physiological
non	opening(s)	participate	physiology
nonenergy	operated	particles	pills
nonofficial	operations	partition(s)	pin
nonprofessional	operative	pass(ed)	pinworm
nonprofit	opposite	(es) (ing)	pitcher
nonstimulating	optic	passage(way)	pituitary
normally	optimal	patch	placement
nose	optional	pathological	plain
nostril(s)	oral(ly)	patient*(s*)	plasma
notch	ordered*	patterns	pleural
notebook	orders*	pause	plug
noted	ordinarily	pectoral	plunged
notice	ordinary	pediatric	pm
notify	organ(ism)	pelvic	pneumonia
nourishment	(isms) (ized) (s)	pelvis	pneumothorax
nowadays	oriented	penicillin	pocket
nucleus	ortho	percent	pointed
nurse*(s)	orthopedic	perforation	policies
nursing	otitis	perform(ed)	polio
nutrients	outer	(s)	polluted
nutrition	outflow	perineal	pons
object(ive)	outlet	periodic	poorly
(s)	output	periods	port
obliged	outward	peripheral	portal
observant	oval	peritoneal	portion
observation	ovaries	permanent	positioned
observe(d)	ovary	permit(ted)	positive
(s)	overhead	perpendicular	possibility
observing	oxidize	persist	postals

posted
posterior(ly)
posture
potions
pounded
pour(ed)
  (ing)
practical
practice(d)
  (s)
practicum
precaution
preceded
precedes
precipitation
precision
predispose
prefer(able)
  (s)
prefix
pregnancy
preigniting
premium
preoperation
preparation
prepare(d)
  (s)
prepping
prescribed
preserve
preset
pressed
pressures
prevent(ative) (ed)
  (ing) (ion) (s)
previous(ly)
primary
prior
privacy
probe
procedure*(s)
proceed
processed
processes
produce(s)

producing
profuse
project
prolonged
promptly
prone
proper(ly)
proportion
protect(ed)
  (ive) (s)
protein(s)
proven
provides
psyche
psychiatric
psychological
psychosis
psychosocial
psychosurgical
pubic
publicized
pulley(s)
pulmonary
pulsation
pulse
pump(ed)
  (s)
punch(ed)
puncture
pupil(s)
purge
purulent
pus
push(ed)
  (ing)
pushbutton
qualification
qualities
quantities
quantity
rack
radial
radiation
radical
radiopaque

raise
ranks
rapid(ly)
rash
rattle
ray(s)
reaching
reactions
reacts
readily
readings
readjustment
realize
rear
reasonable
reasons
reassemble(d)
recall
receptacle
receptors
recognition
recommendation
recommended
recorded
recorder
recordings
records
recovering
recovery
rectal
rectum
recumbent
recurrence
reduce(d)
reestablish
refer(ence)
  (red) (ring)
refill
reflect
reflex
refrigerate
refusal
refuse
regarded
regarding

regardless
regimen
region
registered
registration
regular(ly)
regulated
regulates
regulating
regulation
rehabilitate
rejected
related
relation
relationship
relative(ly)
relax
release(d)
releasing
reliable
relieve(d)
religions
remain(s)
remedies
remote
removable
removal
remove(d)
removing
render
renewing
rented
repaired
repeat
replace(d)
replacing
replenish
reports
represent
reprocessed
reproduction
request(ed)
  (ing)
require(ment)
  (s)

requiring
requisition
resembles
resembling
reserve
reservoir
resident
residual
resist(ant)
(ing)
resources
respects
respiration
respirator
response(s)
responsible
restore(d)
restoring
restrain(ts)
restrict(ed)
resulted
resulting
retained
retardation
retention
reticulum
retina
retroperitoneal
review
rheumatic
rhinitis
rhythmical
rib
ribosomes
ringers
rinse(d)
rinsing
risk
robe
role
roots
rooted
roughage
route(s)
routine

rubella
rudimentary
ruled
rules
ruling
rupture
rural
sac(s)
sacrament(s)
sacrolili
sacrum
safe(ly)
(ty)
saline
salivary
salts
sample(s)
sampling
sanguinous
satisfaction
satisfied
scab
scale(s)
scar(red)
scares
schedule
sciatic
scientists
scopes
screen
screw
sealed
search
seat
sebaceous
secondary
seconds
secretion(s)
sections
select(ed)
(ion)
semi
semiliquid
sensations
sensing

sensitive
sensitivity
sensor
sensorium
sensory
separate(d)
(ly) (s)
Septisol
septum
sequelae
sequential
seriously
serum
severe
severed
shake(s)
shaking
shape(d)
shaved
sheath
sheds
shields
shift(s)
shock(ed)
shortened
shorter
shoulder
showing
shreaded
shrouded
sick(ness)
siderails
sight
sigmoid
sign(ed)
(ing) (s)
signal
signature
significant
sinuses
site*(s)
situations
skeletal
skill(ed)
(ful) (s)

skin*
skull
slack
slept
slight(ly)
sling
sloughs
smear
smell
smoke
smooth(ly)
snapped
sneezing
sniffed
soda
solid
solution(s)
solvent
soma
somatic
sophisticated
sore
source
spare
spasm(s)
speaking
specialize
specialty
specifically
specified
specimen(s)
spectacular
spectrum
spinal
spirits
spiritual
spirochete
sponge
spontaneous
spread(er)
stable
staffed
staffs
standards
standing

stands
stapes
staphylococcal
statistics
status
stays
steady
stenosis
stenotic
sterile
sterility
sterilized
stethoscope
stimulate(d)
stimulating
stimulation
stoma
stomach*
stool(s)
   (ing)
stopper
storage
stored
storeroom
stove
straighten
strain(ing)
   (s)
strands
strata
streptococcus
stretch(er)
   (ers) (es)
strikes
strip
strives
stroke
structors
structure*(s)
studies
stunted
stupor
subclavian
subjective
subsequent

subside
substance(s)
suffer
sufficient
suffix
suggestion
suitable
suited
suites
sum
summary
super
superior
superstition
supervision
supervisor
supine
supplied
supplies
supply
supported
supporting
supports
suprarenal
supreme
surgeon
surgeries
surgery*
surgical
surround(ing)
susceptible
suspected
swab
swallow(ing)
   (s)
swelling
symptomatic
symptoms
synchronize
syndrome
Syntex
synthesize
syringe
systematic
systole

tablets
tape(d)
task
taut
technician
technique(s)
techs
temp.
temporal
tempting
tends
tens
tension
term
terminal
termination
terribly
tertiary
testing
tests
thalamus
therapies
therapy
thermometer
thermostat
thickened
thicker
thigh
thin
thoroughly
thousand(s)
threading
threadlike
threat
thrive
throat
thyroid
tilt
tissue*(s)
title
toe(s)
toenails
tongs
tongue
tooth

towel(s)
toxic
toxins
trachea
tract(ion*)
transfer(red)
transfusion
transient
transmission
transmitted
transport(ation)
transverse
trapped
trauma
traveled
travels
tray
treating
treatments
treelike
triglycerin
trillionth
trimester
trip
trochanter
troughlike
trunk(s)
tube*
tubing
tumor
turning
tympanic
typical
ulcer
ulnar
unauthorized
uncomfortable
uncommunicable
unconstitute
underlies
undernourish
undertaken
undressing
undue
unequivocal

Occupational Literacy Education

unethical	vacoliter	vibrating	watery
unfastened	vacutainer	vibrations	weakening
unfastens	vagina	vicinity	weakness
unique	vaginal	vigorously	wear
unit*(s)	valid	violating	weaving
unlock	valuable	visible	weekly
unnecessary	(s)	vision	weight
unnoticed	valve	visitation	(s)
unpleasant	variations	visiting	wheelchair
unplugged	variety	visitors	wheels
unprotected	vary	vital	whereas
unreasonable	vein	vitamin	whitish
untold	venereal	vocal	widespread
untreated	ventricle(s)	voltage	withdraw
upright	ventricular	voluntary	wither
upset(ting)	verify	volunteers	witnessed
urge	vermicular	vomit	witnessing
urinal	vertebrae	(ing)	wondering
urinary	vertically	voxiderm	worm(s)
urine	vessel(s)	wards	worn
uterine	via	warning	worried
uterus	viability	wash*	worry
utility	vial	waste	worth
vaccine	vibrates	watched	wound

HIGH FREQUENCY WORDS
MACHINE TOOL OPERATOR

ac	diameter	measure	round
base	draw	measuring	scale
cable	(ing)	metal	screw
caliber	eight	meter	sheet
capacitor	elevation	micrometer	shows
check	equal	miter	shunt
circuit	fig.	motor	steel
clamp	fixture	patterns	success
coil	gauge	pick	switch
connected	(s)	pieces	taper
crisis	generator	pipe	tool
degrees	holes	plug	(s)
depth	inch(es)	remove	vertical
develop	machine	rod	voltage

abilities
ability
abnormal
ac*
accident(s)
accomplish
accordance
accuracy
accurate
achieve(ment)
acidic
actual
adaptable
adjust(ment)
adopted
advantage(s)
advent
adverse
advice
affect(s)
align(ment)
allowances
allowed
alternator
altitude
aluminum
ammeter
ampere(s)
analyze
ancient
angle(d)
   (s)
anticipate
anvil
apart
apathetic
appearance
appendices
appliances
application
applies
apply
approximate
arc
armored

arranged
arrangement
aside
assembled
assistance
assistant
associated
attach(ment)
attaining
attempt
attitudes
attracted
attributed
automated
automatically
automobile
avoid(ed)
aware
backout
balance(d)
ballast
base*(s)
battery
bearing(s)
behavior*
bellhousing
biological
bisect(ing)
   (ors)
bit
blade
blanks
blew
block
bobbin
bolt
bore(d)
boring
boss
bottle
branch(es)
breaker
breaking
bushings
buyer

cable*
calibrating
centers
centrifugal
characteristic
charged
charges
charter
chased
check*(ed)
   (ing)
cheek
chimney
choosing
circle(s)
circuit*(s)
circulate(s)
circumference
clamp*
classification
clean(ing)
clearance
cleats
code
coil*(s)
coincides
collar
collision
columns
combination
compared
compass
compensate
completed
completing
complex
compliment
composition
compound(ed)
compressor
computer
concentrate
condition(ed)
   (ing)
conduct(or)

cone
connect(ed*)
   (ing) (ion) (or)
   (ors) (s)
consecutive
consist(ent)
   (s)
constant
constructed
constructing
contact
contained
container(s)
continuous
contribute
controlled
controls
convenience
convenient
conversion
copper
cord(s)
core
corners
corrected
correspond
corridor
costly
counter
creates
crises
crisis*
crisscross
critical
crosses
cured
curved
custom
cutting
cycle(s)
cylinder(s)
damage
damp
danger(ous) (s)
decimal(s)

deck
decrease
defining
definite(ly)
degrees*
denominator
depend(ent)
(ing) (s)
depth*
derived
describe
designer
desired
detect
determine
develop*(ing)
(s)
device(s)
diagonal(ly)
diameter*(s)
diamond
die
dielectric
differ(ently)
diminsion(s)
directions
disagreement
disassociate
discharges
disconnect
discovered
discussed
discusses
discussing
disintegrate
disorder
disputable
distance
distinct
distinguish
distructed
disturbed
divide
divisible
divisions

draftsman
drain
draw*(ing*)
(n) (s)
dress
drill(ed)
driver
drives
driving
drop(ped)
duct
dynamic
effectively
effectiveness
eight*
(een)
(hs) (y)
elbow(s)
electric(al)
(ian)
(ity)
electromagnet*
electrostatic
elevation*
eleven
emphasis
employed
enclosed
ended
ends
energized
energy
engage(s)
engines
enhances
enters
environment
equal*(ized)
(s)
equipped
equivalent
erase
erect
essence
essential(ly)

establish
etc.
evaluates
evenly
eventually
evident
exactly
examples
excel
executive
exert
existing
expanded
expense
expensive
experience*
experiencing
experiment
expert
explain(ed)
exposed
expression
extend
extension
extensive(ly)
exterior
external
extra
extremely
faced
factor
failure
familiar
farad
fashioned
fastened
fault
favor(able)
feed
fields
fifteen
fifty
fig.*
figured
filed

financial
finer
finish(ed)
fit(ted)
(ting)
fix(ed)
(ture*) (tures)
fluctuating
flux
focus
forced
four way
fours
fourth
fractional
fractions
frame(s)
frequently
frictional
frustrated
frustrating
functional
functioning
fuse(d)
gable
gallon
gases
gassed
gauge*(s*)
gear
generated
generator*(s)
glandular
gradual
graduated
graduation
greatest
grind(er)
groove
grounded
grounding
grow(s)
guard(s)
guess
guide(lines)

guy	inductor	levers	milliampere
habits	influence(s)	lifetime	mini
hammer	inner	limit(s)	minor
handle(d)	inquiry	linear	minute
handling	inserted	liquid	mishandled
handout	inspecting	load(ed)	misused
happen(s)	inspection	(ing) (s)	miter*(s)
hardened	installation	locate(d)	model
harm	instance(s)	locating	modify
hazard	instant	location(s)	moldings
heads	instructor	locator	molecules
heat(ed)	instrument	lock(ed)	momentary
(ing)	insulation	(ing)	momentum
heel	insulator	logical	motor*(s)
height	insurance	loss(es)	mounted
hide	intense	lowest	multiple
highest	intensity	machine*(s)	nearby
highly	interact(ion)	machining	necessarily
holds	interchange	machinist(s)	negative
hole(s*)	intermediate	magnet(ic)	neutral
homes	internal	(s)	nine(ty)
horizontal	interrupted	magnetism	numbered
horsepower	intersect(ed)	magnetized	numerators
household	(ion)	máintain(ed)	numerous
humor	interwoven	manager	obtain(ing)
identified	invention	manufacture	occupation
identity(ing)	involve(ment)	mark(ed)	occurs
illustrate	(s)	materials	octagon
imbalance	irregular	math	offers
immeasurable	jacket	maximum	officials
immediately	jarred	measure*(d)	offset(ting)
improperly	jarring	(ment) (ing*)	oil
improved	join(t)	mechanical	older
inability	judging	mechanism	opening(s)
inaccurate	keeper	medium	operate
incessantly	knurled	mental*(ly)	operations
inch*(es*)	lapped	mercury	operator
included	lathe(s)	message	opposite
includes	leakage	metal*	oridinary
increases	leg(s)	meter*(s)	original
increasing	legal	metric	outer
independent	lengths	microampere	outlet(s)
index	lessen	micrometer*	outline
indicates	lesser	microphone	output
induce	leverage	mill(ing) (s)	overheat

overlapping	processes	remodeling	screw*(ed)
oxygen	produced	remove*	(s)
pace	profile(s)	repelling	scribed
panel	project(ing)	repetition	script
papers	(ion)	replaced	sealed
parallel	proper(ly)	represent	seam
patterns*	protect(ion)	(ation)	secondary
perception	(ive)	(ed) (s)	sections
permit(s)	provides	require(ment)	secure
perpendicular	quarter	(s)	security
phase(s)	quick(ly)	resetting	seek(ing)
physically	radius	resistance	seethe
physiological	raised	resolve	segments
pick*(ed)	rapid(ly)	resolving	seizing
pieces*	rated	resources	seldom
pilots	react	respective	semicircle
pipe*(s)	readily	respond(s)	semidiameter
pivots	readings	responsible	semiprofile
planers	ream	resulting	senses
planes	rebuilt	reverse(d)	sensory
plate(s)	receive	reversing	separate
plug*(s)	recess	review	separating
pole(s)	(es)	revolution	separation
porcelain	recognize(s)	ridiculous	separators
portable	recognizing	ring(s)	seventy
portion	recorder	rod*(s)	severe
positive	rectangular	rolled	shape(s)
potential	reduce	rotation	sharp
pound(s)	reduction	rough	shield
practice	reevaluation	round*	shipping
preceded	refer(s)	row	shock(ed)
precision	refrigerate	rpm	shop
predict	regardless	rule	shoulder
preferred	registered	runs	showing
preheat(s)	regrind	safely	shows*
preliminary	regular	safety	shunt*(s)
prepare	regulate	sample	signal
presented	regulating	satisfied	signed
prevent	regulator	satisfies	significant
previous	related	satisfy	sill
primarily	relation(ship)	savings	similarly
principles	relatively	scale*	simultaneous
printed	release	scientists	sixteenth(s)
probability	relying	scoop(s)	sixty
proceed	remedied	screen	sized

sizes	stick	tester	unpleasant
skid	stimuli	theories	upper
skilled	stimulus	thereby	vacation
skim	stops	thimble	valve
slick	stored	thirty	variation
slides	storing	throttle	varied
slight(ly)	strengths	thrown	varies
sling	strictly	tickets	variety
sloppy	striking	title	vary(ing)
slots	strip	tolerance	vernier
slotted	struggling	(s)	versus
socket(s)	strung	tolerate	vertical*
soft	stud	tolerating	viewed
solid	substance	tool*(s*)	volt(age*)
solution	substitute	(room)	(s)
solve(d)	success*(ful)	torque	volumes
solving	surge	totaled	wait
sounding	suspended	trace(d)	waste
source	switch*(es)	transfer	watt(s)
spaces	symmetrical	transition	weakened
spare	synchronous	transmission	wear(ing)
speaking	synonymous	transmitted	weights
specifically	tables	treated	weld(er)
speed(s)	tangent	triangle(s)	wheel(s)
spend	tape	trigger	whereas
spin	taper*(ed)	trip	width
spindle(s)	(ing) (s)	truck(ing)	wind
splice(d)	taping	(s)	wire
(s)	taps	trust	wiring
split	task(s)	turning	wise
squared	taut	turns	withdrawal
stages	telescopic	turret	workable
stamped	tempered	twentieth	worker
standards	tend(s)	twenty	(s)
starter(s)	tension	twisted	worn
starting	terminal(s)	unit(s)	wound
starts	terminated	(y)	wrapper
steel*	tested	unknowns	zero

HIGH FREQUENCY WORDS
SECRETARY

address	credit	learn	regular
administrate	curriculum	libraries	remission
alphabetic	date	library	request
application	director	mail	resources
appropriate	edge	management	responsible
approval	employee(s)	materials	rules
approved	excused	memorandum	semester
arrangement	extended	objectives	serve
assistant	fee(s)	officer	signed
attendance	file	participate	storage
carbon	filing	permission	supervisor
card	fill	personnel	supply
clerical	film	please	thinner
communicate	folder	principal	touch
conference	guides	procedure	transportation
contact	included	profession	travel
coordinator	index	proper	trip(s)
copies	initials	proposal	typing
copy	instruction	recommendation	unit
courses	lacquer	records	write

Occupational Literacy Education

TECHNICAL VOCABULARY
SECRETARY

abbreviate
abbreviation
abilities
ability
abroad
absence
academic
acceptable
access(ion)
accidents
accommodate
accompany
accomplish
accordance
accountant
accounting
accustomed
achieve
acknowledge
acquisition
active(ly)
adding
addition
address*(ee)
 (ing)
adequate
adjunct
adjusting
administer
administrate*
admire
admissions
admit(ted)
adopt(ed)
advance(d)
advantages
adversely
advisors
affected
agencies
agency
agents
agreed
agreement
aids

aims
aligned
alignment
alleged
allotted
allowance
allowed
allowing
allows
alphabet(ic*)
alternated
amended
analyze
angles
announcement
anticipate
anticipation
apostrophe
apparent
appearing
appears
appendix
applicable
applicants
application*
applies
apply(ing)
appointment
appreciable
appropriate*
approval*
approved*
approves
approving
aptitude
archival
archives
arise
arrange(ment*)
arrival
artisans
aside
aspect(s)
assembly
assessed

assessment
assigned
assignment
assist(ance)
 (ant*) (s)
associate
assume
assumption
assurance
assure
assuring
attempt
attend(ance*)
 (s)
attorney
attributes
audio
 (visual)
audit(ing)
augment
author
automatic
avoid(ing)
award
baggage
balance
band
basically
bear(ing)
becomes
begin
behavior
believed
benefit(s)
biased
bids
biweekly
blank
block
blower
bonds
bookkeeping
books
borrowed
boss

bulletin
bureau
bursar
business(es)
byproducts
calculated
cancel(ed)
 (ing)
capabilities
caption
carbon*
card*(s)
 (board)
carrier(s)
carries
carry
carton(s)
cassette
catalog(ing)
 (s)
centered
centers
certificate
certified
certify
channels
characteristic
chargeable
charged
charges
charts
check(ed)
 (ing)
chemical
chip
chosen
chronological
circulation
circumstances
citation
classification
classified
classify
clerical*
clerk

clients
code(d)
cognizant
collection
colon
combined
combines
comma
commerce
commercial
commitment
communicate*
companies
compared
compatible
competence
competition
complaints
completed
completing
completion
complex
compliment
component(s)
compound
comprehensive
comprises
computer
computing
concepts
conclusion
concrete
condition
conduct
conference*
confirmed
conflict
confuse
confusion
connected
connecting
conscious
consecutive
consent
consequence

considerable
considerate
considering
consistent
construed
consult(ed)
  (ing)
contact*
container(s)
containing
contests
continually
continuing
continuous
contraction
contracts
contractual
convenience
cooperative
coordinator*
copies*
copy*(ing)
cord
corporation
correct(ly)
correspond
courses*
coverage
covered
created
creation
credit*
critical
crumpling
cultural
cultures
current
curricular
curriculum*
customer
danger
dash
date*(d)
  (s)
dealt

dear*
decide
decimal
declared
decrease
deemed
defined
defines
definition
delivery
demand
demonstrate
departure
depend(ing)
  (s)
depicts
description
designate(s)
designer(s)
desired
desiring
desk
destroy(ed)
detailed
details
detect
determiner
determines
detract
detrimental
develop(ing)
diagonal
dictate
dictating
dictation
dictionaries
dictionary
differentiate
diploma
directed
directions
director*(s)
  (y)
disadvantage
disapproval

disapproving
disc
discarded
discern
discontinuous
discriminate
discuss(ed)
displays
disposal
disposing
distinctive
distribute
distribution
divide
divisions
doubtful
duplicate
duplicating
duration
duties
earns
ease
easily
economical
edge*(s)
educational
educator
effectiveness
efficiency
efficiently
electronic
eligibility
eligible
emergencies
emphasis
employed
employee*(s*)
employer
employing
employment
encompass
encourage(d)
engaged
enhance
enlightened

SECRETARY (continued)

enrich
enroll(ed)
   (ing) (ment) (s)
enterprise
entrusted
envelope(s)
equipped
equivalent
errors
establish(ing)
etc.
etiquette
evaluated
evaluation
event(s)
exact
examination
examiners
examples
excellent
exception(s)
excess
excused*
executive
exhaust
exist
expanded
expecting
expects
expense(s)
expensive
explain(ed)
extended*
extends
extension
extra(s)
extreme
facilities
factor(s)
factory
familiar
faults
feasible
features
federally

fee*(s*)
file*(d)
   (s)
filing*
fill*(ed)
film*
financial
firmly
firms
flammability
flammable
flaws
folder*(s)
follow up
forwarded
fourth
framework
frequent(ly)
fulltime
fully
functions
gained
gallon
geographic
goal(s)
governed
governing
grade(d)
graduate(d)
grammatical
granted
graphics
graphs
guarantees
guidance
guide
guideline(s)
guiding
handling
handwriting
happen
harassment
hazardous
heading
headquarters

headset
helping
hesitate
highly
hired
hiring
holder
holdings
holds
homes
hone
hourly
hub
hyphen(ated)
   (ation)
identical
identification
identified
identifies
identify(ing)
illustrate
illustrating
illustrator
implementation
implies
improve(d)
   (ment)
improving
inactive
inadvisable
inch
included*
includes
incorrectly
increases
indefinite
independent
index*(ing)
indicate(s)
indicating
indication
indicator
indirect
inferior
influences

inform
   (al)
inhalation
initial(s*)
initiated
insert(ed)
inspect(ion)
institutes
instruction*
instructor
insurance
insured
integrated
intended
intense
intent
intercom
interested
interfere(nce)
interoffice
interpretation
interstate
interview(s)
inventory
investigate
invitation
involves
involving
isolated
item(ized)
itinerary
joint(ly)
jurisdiction
justification
juvenile
label(s)
lacquer*
laundry
lawyer(s)
leading
learn*(ing)
legal
legitimate
letterhead
levels

libraries*
library*
lifting
likelihood
limit(ed)
liquid
listed
listings
locally
located
location(s)
lodging
logical
machine(ry)
  (s)
mail*(ing)
maintain(ed)
  (ing) (s)
manage(ment*)
  (r)
manual(ly)
margin
mark(ed)
  (er) (s)
materials*
maximum
measure(ment)
  (s)
media
meetings
memorandum*
memorize
memory
mention(ed)
merchandise
merit
message
microfilm
microforms
microrecord
mimeograph
minimum
minute
miscellaneous
misfiled

misfiling
misspelled
misunderstood
mixed
motion
multiply
mutual
narrow
necessarily
necessity
neglect
negligence
nondiscriminate
normally
notations
noticeable
notification
notify(ing)
noxious
numbered
numeric(ally)
numerous
objectives*
obscured
obtain(ing)
occasion
occupation
occupies
occupy
occur
offer(ed)
  (ings) (s)
officer*
offices
official
offset
omit
ongoing
opening
operated
operator
optional
ordered
orderly
orders

ordinarily
ordinary
organized
organizer
orientation
orienting
origin
original
outcomes
outline(d)
overall
overhead
overlook
overnight
overtime
paced
packages
parentheses
partial
participant(s)
participate*
particles
partners
pass
payable
payment
percent(age)
perfection
perform(ing)
periodic(al)
periods
permanent(ly)
permission*
permitted
personally
personnel*
pertaining
petition
philosophy
photograph
phrase(s)
pictured
pictures
placement
placing

planned
please*
pleasure
policies
portable
portion
positions
positive
postal
practical(ly)
practice
precaution
preceding
predetermine
preface
preferred
prefixes
preliminary
premises
prepare(d)
  (s)
preservation
pressboard
presuppose
prevent(s)
primarily
primary
principal*(s)
principles
printouts
prior(ities)
privileges
procedure*(s*)
processing
producers
product(ivity)
profession*
programed
project(ion)
  (s)
promotion
pronounced
proof
proper*(ly)
proposal(s)

proposed*	referring	schedule(d)	speaking
protect(ion)	refiled	(s)	specialist
prove	reform	scholar	specialize
provides	refrigerate	sciences	specialities
providing	refund	script	specifically
provisions	regarding	sealed	specified
publication	region(al)	searcher	spelled
punctuation	registered	seats	spelling
pupil(s*)	registers	secondary	spending
purchase	registrar	secretarial	sponsored
purchasing	registration	sectional	sponsors
purposes	regular*(ly)	sections	spouse(s)
purposive	regulated	secure(d)	staffed
qualification	regulation	security	stamped
qualified	regulator	selection	stamps
qualify	reimbursement	semester*(s)	standards
quantities	requires	semicolon	standpoint
quarter	requisition	seminar(s)	stapler
quick	resemblance	sender	static
quotation	reserve	sending	status
quoted	resident	sentence(s)	stimulating
radius	resource(s*)	separate(ly)	stocks
rapidly	respective	sequence	storage*
rarely	response	serve*(s)	store(d)
rates	responsible*	session(s)	storing
reaches	restriction	setting	stress(ed)
reader(s)	retaining	sign(ed*)	stripes
reality	retention	(ing)	strips
reasonable	retired	signal	studies
receipt	retrieval	signature(s)	styles
receive	returning	significant	subcontract
receiving	returns	signify	subdivided
recognize	review(ed)	sincere(ly)	subdivision
recommend(ation)	(ing)	situations	subjects
(ed)	reward	skilled	submission
recordings	ridding	skills	submitted
records*	rival	slash	subscribe
recreation	role	slight	subsequent
reduce(d)	routes	slip(s)	substitute
reducing	rule(s*)	smudges	substitution
reduction	salary	smudging	subsystem(s)
reference(s)	salutation	solve	succeeding
referencing	satisfaction	sought	success
referral(s)	satisfactory	spaces	sufficient
referred	satisfy	sparingly	suggested

suggestion	text	uncertain	visible
superintendent	thoughtful	(ty)	visiting
superior	thoughts	underlies	visitor
supervise	title(s)	underneath	visual(s)
supervisor*	totally	understood	vocabulary
supplies	touch*	undertaking	void
supply*	toxic(ity	unexcused	volumes
supporting	trades	unique	wage(s)
suppose	transfer(red)	unit*(s)	weight
suspects	translucent	unjustifiable	widely
suspicions	transmitted	unless	wider
suspicious	transparent	unusual	width
systematic	transportation	utilization	willful
tab(bed)	travel*	utilized	winter
(s)	trend(s)	vacation	wishes
takes	trip*(s*)	valuable	wishing
tape(d)	truly	valued	withdrawing
target	trustees	van	workable
tasks	tuition	varies	workplace
teacher(s)	typed	variety	workshop
telegram	typewriter	vastly	wrinkle
telephone	typewriting	vendor	(d)
temporarily	typical	verified	wrinkling
temporary	ultimate	verify	write*(rs)
tendency	unable	viewer	(s)
terminate(d)	unacceptable	violation	yesterday
testing	unbroken	visa	yours

Occupational Literacy Education

HIGH FREQUENCY WORDS
WELDER

ac	electric	metal	root
acetylene	electrode(s)	meter	shock
angle	flame	motor	shows
arc	flat	natural	shunt
argon	flow	oxygen	speed
base	fusion	pass	starting
bead	gas	penetration	steel
burn	gauges	phone	switch(es)
cable	generator(s)	pipe	tape
carbon	heat	plate(s)	tip(s)
circuit	horizontal	polarity	torch
coil	hose	pole	travel
connected	inch	produce(d)	unit
copper	iron	properties	valve
correct	joint(s)	puddle	voltage
cutting	lamp	resistance	weld(ed)
dc	load	reverse	(ing)
degrees	magnet(ic)	rod(s)	wire

TECHNICAL VOCABULARY
WELDER

abbreviate
absorbs
ac*
accessible
accidental
accomplish
accounts
accumulate
acetone
acetylene*
acidic
acting
acts
actual
adapted
add
address
adjust(ment)
advantage(s)
advisable
affected
affects
airplanes
alignment
allow(ed)
 (ing)
alloys
alternating
alternator
aluminum
ammeter
amounts
ampere(s)
analyze
angle*(s)
apart
appearance
appliances
application
appreciation
appropriate
approved
approximate
arc*(ing)
argon*

armored
arrange(ment)
arrow
asbestos
associated
atmosphere
atmospheric
atomic
attach
attempt(ing)
attracted
automatic
avoid(ed)
backfire
backing
backup
balanced
ballast
band
bar(s)
bare
base*
bath
battery
bead*(s)
bearings
beat
bellhousing
bessemer
beveled
bit
bite
blank
blow
bobbin
booklet
boss
bottom
bought
box(es)
brass
braze(d)
brazing
break(er)
 (ing)

breathe
brick
bridge
broken
bronze
buddy
build(up)
built
bulb
burn*(ed)
 (ing) (s) (t)
buttons
buy(ing)
buzz
cable*(s)
cadmium
calcium
calibrated
calls
cam
canvas
capacitance
capacitor*
capacity
carbon*
card(s)
careful
carpet
carries
carry(ing)
carved
cassette
cast(ings)
cat
catch
category
cathode(s)
caused
causes
ceiling
centerline
centrifugal
chain
chamber
chances

chancing
characteristic
charged
charging
charges
chart
check
chemical(ly)
chill
chipping
circuit*(s)
circulate
clamping
clap
classes
classification
clean(ed)
 (er)
clearance
cleats
clockwise
clogged
coated
coating
code
coil*(s)
collect
colorless
column
combination
combines
combining
combustion
commercial
commutator
compensate
completed
complicate
composed
composition
compound(ed)
 (s)
compress(ed)
 (or)
computer

Occupational Literacy Education

concentrate
condition(ed)
  (ing)
conduct(ive) (or)
cone
confined
confused
connect(ed*)
  (ing) (ion) (or)
  (ors) (s)
constant
constricted
constructed
construction
consumable
contact
contained
container
containing
contaminate
continuous
contour
contraction
controlled
controls
convention
conversation
cool(ed)
  (er) (s)
copper*
cords
core(d)
correct*(ly)
coupling'
cover(s)
crack(s)
crane
crosses
crowbar
crowned
cubic
cuff
currently
custom(ary)
cutting*

cycles
cylinder(s)
damage
dangerous
dc*
debt
decimal
deck
decrease
defective
definite
degrees*
demonstrate
densities
density
depend(ing)
  (s)
deposit(ing)
deposition
depth
designer
desirable
desired
destroys
detail
develops
device(s)
dial
diameter
dielectric
directed
disadvantage
discharges
disconnect
discrepancy
dissolved
dissolving
disturbed
divided
divisible
downhill
downward
draftsman
drag
drawing(s)

drill(ed)
ductility
duty
ease
easier
eats
economical
edge(s)
efficient(ly)
elbow(s)
electric*(al)
  (ian) (ity)
electrode*(s*)
electromagnet
electrons
electrostatic
eliminates
employed
employer
encountered
ends
energized
energy
engine(s)
engineering
enters
equal(ized)
  (s)
equivalent
essence
essential(ly)
establish
evenly
event(ually)
evident
exactly
examples
exceed
excess(ive)
exert
exhaust
existing
exists
expansion
explanatory

explosion(s)
explosive
exposed
expressed
extend
extensively
external
extreme(ly)
fabricating
facets
factor
failure
fairly
fashioned
fast(ened)
  (er) (est)
fatal
fault(s)
feather
feature(s)
fed
ferrous
fields
fifth
fig.
figured
filler
fillet
finest
fitted
fittings
fixed
fixtures
flame*
flameout
flammable
flare
flashback
flat*
flex(ible)
flints
flouride
flow*
fluctuating
flush

flux(es)
forex
forged
formation
formed
formulate
fourfold
fours
fourway
fractional
fracture
frequency
frequently
friction(al)
fuel
fumes
furnace
fuse(s)
fusion*
gage
galvanized
gap
gas*
gasfed
gauge(s*)
generated
generator*(s*)
glare
goggles
gouging
grade(s)
grease(r)
greatest
grind(ers)
(ing)
grip
grooved
grounded
grounding
guards
guess
guide
halfway
hammer
handier

handle(d)
hang
hardening
hardest
harm
haul
hazard
hearing
hearth
heat*(ed)
(ing)
heavier
helium
helper
helpful
hibond
highcarbon
highest
highly
highpressure
highspeed
highstrength
hissing
Hobart(s)
holder(s)
holds
hopper
horizontal*
horsepower
horseshoe
hose*(s)
household
hydrogen
identical
identification
ignite
immediately
impossible
improperly
impurities
inaccurate
inch*(es)
inclusions
incoming
incorrect

increases
indicate(s)
indicating
indication
induce
inductor
inherent
initial
initiates
inner
innovation
input
inspect(ed)
(ion)
installation
instance
instant
instructor
insulation
insulator
insure
intend(ed)
intense
intensity
interchange
intercom
intermittant
interrupted
invented
invention
involves
ionizes
iron*
items
jarred
jarring
join(ed)
(ing)
joint*(s*)
keeper
key
kicks
killed
kindling
kink

laboratory
lamp*(s)
lap
largely
latent
layer
laying
leak(age)
(ing) (s)
leaves
leaving
lecture
leg(s)
lenses
lesser
lever(age)
lightweight
limit(s)
liquifying
litre
load*(er)
(ing) (s)
located
locations
machinable
machine(d)
(s)
magnesium
magnet*(s)
magnetic*
magnetism
magnetized
maintained
maintenance
manganese
manually
manufacture
materials
max
maximum
measure(d)
(ment) (ing)
mechanical
mechanism

melt(ed)
(ing) (s)
mercury
metal*(s)
meter*(s)
metre
metric
microampere
microwire
mild
millimeter
milling
mishandled
mistake
model
moderately
modernized
modify
molecules
motion
motor*(s)
mounted
movable
multiple
narrow
naturally
nearby
negative
neutral*
nipple(s)
nonburnable
nondestruct
nonferrous
nonpressure
notice
nozzle
nut
obtain
occupation
occur(s)
odorless
offers
oil*(y)
openings
operate(d)

operating
operations
operator
opposite
ordinarily
ordinary
ore
orifice
original
otherwise
outlet(s)
output
outstripped
oval
overall
overhead
overheat(ing)
overmatch
overseas
oxidation
oxides
oxidize(d)
oxyacetylene
oxygen*
panel
parallel
partially
partner
pass*(es)
(ing)
patch
path
peculiar
penetrate
penetration*
percent
perform(ed)
permanent
permit(s)
phase(s)
phone*
physically
pick(er)
(up)
pictures

pieces
pig
pin
pinpoint
pipe*(s)
pitched
pivots
plate*(s*)
plug(s)
plus
pocket(ed)
(s)
poisonous
polarity*
pole*
porcelain
porosity
portable
positioned
positions
positive
pot
potential
practice
preceding
preferable
preference
preferred
preheat(ing)
(s)
preionizes
preparation
prepared
presents
pressures
prevent(ed)
(s)
primarily
primary
principal
procedure
proceed
processes
prod
produce*(d*) (s)

progressive
projection
prone
proper(ly)
properties*
proportion
protect(ed)
(ion) (ive)
provides
publication
puddle*
pull(ed)
pumps
purchased
pure
purify
purity
qualified
ranging
rapid(ly)
rapidity
rated
readily
realize
rebuilt
receive
recommended
recorder(s)
recovering
rectangular
reduce(d)
reels
refer(s)
reference
refrigerate
registration
regular
regulator(s)
reinforcement
related
relationship
relatively
relight(ing)
relying
removable

remove(d)
repair(ed)
repelling
require(ment)
  (s)
reset
resin
resistance*
resists
respiration
respirator
resulting
reverse*(d)
reversible
reversing
review
rich
ricochet
rivet
rod*(s)
root*
rotating
rotation
route
rpm
rugged
ruin
sampling
saturated
scale
scattered
scrap
scratched
screw(ed)
seamless
seat
secured
security
select
semester
semiautomate
separate
separation
setting
settle

settling
severe
sewing
shape(s)
sharp
sheet
shield(ed)
  (ing)
shipping
shipyard
shock*(ed)
shows*
shrill
shrinkage
shunt*(s)
shut
signed
silicon
sill
sink
situations
sizes
slag(ging)
slight(ly)
slip
socket(s)
soldering
solid(s)
soot
sorter
source
spacing
sparks
spatter
specifically
specification
specified
specify
specs
speech
speed*(s)
splice(d)
  (r) (s)
spontaneous
stability

stabilization
stable
stainless
stall
stamped
stamps
standing
starter(s)
starting*
steel(s)
storage
store(d)
  (s)
storing
straighten
strengths
striking
string(er)
strip(s)
strongest
strongly
structural
struggling
strung
subjected
submerged
submerging
substitute
suitable
supplier(s)
supplies
supply
surfaces
surfacing
surge
suspended
switch*(es*)
symbol(s)
synchronous
tack(ing)
tank(s)
tape*
taps
taut
technically

technique
tee
tensile
tension
terminal(s)
terminated
testing
thermal
thicker
thickness(es)
thirds
thorough
threads
tinning
tip*
torch*(es)
track
transfer(red)
transmit(ted)
transport
travel*
trigger
trimmer
tube(s)
tubing
tungsten
twisted
twists
typically
unbroken
unconstitute
undercutting
underneath
unit*(s)
unstable
upright
utility
valve*(s)
varied
varies
variety
vary(ing)
vectors
vee
ventilation

WELDER (continued)

version

vertical

vice

violent

visible

volt(age*) (s)

watt(s)

weakened

wear

weaved

weight

weld* (ed*) (er)

   (ers) (ing*) (s)

wider

wind

wire*(s)

wiring

workplace

worn

wound

woven

wrapped

zero

zinc